Sometimes an Art

Sometimes an Art

NINE ESSAYS ON HISTORY

Bernard Bailyn

ALFRED A. KNOPF   NEW YORK 2015

THIS IS A BORZOI BOOK
PUBLISHED BY ALFRED A. KNOPF

Copyright © 2015 by Bernard Bailyn

All rights reserved.
Published in the United States by Alfred A. Knopf,
a division of Random House LLC, New York,
and distributed in Canada by Random House of Canada
Limited, Toronto, Penguin Random House companies.

www.aaknopf.com

Knopf, Borzoi Books, and the colophon are registered
trademarks of Random House LLC.

Original published data can be found on page 261.

Library of Congress Cataloging-in-Publication Data
Bailyn, Bernard.
Sometimes an art: nine essays on history /
by Bernard Bailyn. —First edition.
pages cm
"This is a Borzoi book"—Title page verso.
Includes bibliographical references and index.
ISBN 978-1-101-87447-9 (hardcover)—ISBN 978-1-101-87448-6 (eBook)
1. History—Philosophy. 2. Historiography—Philosophy.
3. Great Britain—Colonies—Historiography. 4. United
States—Historiography. I. Title.
D16.8.B285 2015
907.2—dc23   2014022229

Jacket design by Oliver Munday

Manufactured in the United States of America
First Edition

for

REBECCA AND DIJANA,

JANE AND SAVA MARIE

Contents

Preface

This is a volume of essays most of which might properly be described as occasional in that they were written in response to invitations on particular occasions. In each case, however, my host allowed me to write freely about the topic at hand, and beyond, at my own discretion. I took advantage of such opportunities to develop my ideas in two areas: the problems and nature of history as a craft, at times an art, and aspects of the history of the colonial peripheries of the early British empire. In both areas I have written elsewhere, but the opportunities offered by these occasions allowed me to isolate key aspects of the broader story and probe them more deeply than I could otherwise have done.

The essays are reprinted as they first appeared except for minor revisions, omissions for sharper focus and greater clarity, and the reduction of references to the immediate occasions. Identification of the place and date of the original publications and the annotation appear in the back matter. In a few cases, I have added to the endnotes, in brackets, brief comments on how the subject has developed in the years that followed the appearance of the essays.

B.B.

PART ONE

On History and
the Struggle to Get It Right

I

Considering the Slave Trade

History and Memory*

I have been wondering about some way to express the importance of the Du Bois Institute slave trade database. Perhaps by analogy. Astronomers knew of the vast range of cosmic phenomena before the Hubble Space Telescope existed, but that extraordinarily

---

* These comments concluded the conference on the Du Bois Trans-Atlantic Slave Trade Database held in Williamsburg, Virginia, in 1998. Since then work on the database has continued, and the updated version is now available online—along with related essays, maps, and other resources—at http://slavevoyages.org. The number of slave voyages included in the database has now risen to thirty-five thousand, accounting for the forced migration of more than twelve million Africans between 1514 and 1866, a million more than were estimated at the time of the conference in 1998. The team that created the database included David Eltis, Emory University; David Richardson, Hull University, England; Stephen Behrendt, now at Wellington University, New Zealand; and Herbert Klein, Columbia University. For recent studies of the database, see Eltis and Richardson, eds., *Extending the Frontier: Essays on the New Transatlantic Slave Trade Database* (New Haven, Conn., 2008).

The papers referred to in these comments were presented at that conference and have been published in the *William and Mary Quarterly*, 3rd ser., 58, no. 1, "New Perspectives on the Transatlantic Slave Trade," January 2001. Quotations from the individual papers are identified in endnotes as they appear in the *Quarterly*.

perceptive eye, coursing freely above the earth's atmosphere, has led to a degree of precision and a breadth of vision never dreamed of before and has revealed, and continues to reveal, not only new information but also new questions never broached before.

So the Du Bois slave trade database, with its tracings of 27,233 Atlantic slave trade voyages, three-quarters of which succeeded in disembarking slaves in the Americas, representing more than two-thirds of all Atlantic slave voyages, has made possible a precision and breadth of documentation in the history of the African diaspora no one had thought possible before and raises a host of new questions.

And also, it must be said, the database suffered glitches in its development not unlike those that afflicted the space telescope. Just as the Hubble's lens proved faulty and had to be repaired before it had the expected clarity, so the CD-ROM on which the slave trade data were first inscribed needed months, even years, of adjustment and correction before it reached the state of accuracy and procedural clarity it now has. At its first public appearance, at Harvard's Atlantic History Workshop in April 1998, the CD-ROM itself could not be used at all, since it was still being cobbled together somewhere in Colorado, and so for that initial public performance the resourceful authors of the database had to funnel the data through an SPSS program, the relation of which to the nonperforming CD-ROM only they understood. Nevertheless, the news, or some of it, came through that computerized squint clearly enough. The sheer scope and comprehensiveness of the database became vivid even then. Now the updated, computerized compilation, with its data susceptible of subtle analysis, is publicly available. While the information it contains is not complete, as the compilers candidly explain (it is, for example, fuller on the British data than on the Portuguese, stronger on the eighteenth century than on the seventeenth), it is yet a record so full, so flexible in its manipulation, and so precise in what it contains that the whole subject, not only of the trade in slaves but slavery itself—its African origins, its demography and ethnography, its economy, its politics, and its role in the development of the Western Hemisphere—has been transformed. The exploitation of this resource has just begun, and as the authors show time and again, there are as yet as many questions as answers.

What strikes one first in reading the papers drawn from the database is the sheer force of numbers. I recall the first crude effort at such quantification many years ago—it was merely punch-card tabulations—and I marvel at how sophisticated the numerical calculations can be and at what can now be perceived just by assembling the numbers.

For numbers (if I may put it this way) count. There is much that numbers alone, sheer quantities, can reveal.

It matters that the overall magnitude of the African diaspora is now quite definitely known: that, as David Eltis explains, it is a fact that eleven million Africans were forcibly carried abroad, more than nine million of them to the Americas. It matters—it stretches the imagination to visualize—that at the height of the British slave trade, in the 1790s, one large slave vessel left England for Africa every other day. It matters that slave rebellions occurred on approximately 10 percent of all slave ships, that 10 percent of the slaves on such voyages were killed in the insurrections (which totals one hundred thousand deaths, 1500–1867), and that the fear of insurrection increased shipboard staffing and other expenses on the Middle Passage by 18 percent, costs that if invested in enlarged shipments would have led to the enslavement of one million more Africans than were actually forced into the system over the course of the long eighteenth century. It matters that the incidence of revolts did not increase with the decline in crew size, hence that slave-centered factors determined the uprisings. It matters that shore-based attacks on European slave ships were twenty times more likely in the Senegal and Gambia River areas than elsewhere in Atlantic Africa. It matters that shipboard mortality (only 50 percent of all slave deaths—the rest occurred in Africa or at embarkation) did *not* increase with the length of the voyages or with the number of slaves per ship ("tighter packing") but *did* vary according to African ports of departure. It matters that French slave ships left Africa with an average load of close to 320 captives; that one such vessel sailed with 900 slaves; that another lost 408 Africans on a single Atlantic voyage; that 92 percent of the "cargo" on another French vessel were children; and that the average number of captives on French vessels rose from 261 in the seventeenth century to 340 at the end of the eighteenth century. It is astonishing simply to attempt to visualize the consequences of the fact that in one year, 1790, French ships landed at least forty thousand slaves on the small island of Saint-Domingue (Haiti), nineteen thousand of them (equal to the entire population of eighteenth-century Boston) at the small port of Cap-Français—and to consider the profound effect that fact must have had.

The numbers are simply in themselves striking, signals of profound human experiences. At its crest, the British slave trade merchants built fifteen to twenty thousand shipboard "platforms" (racks for the confinement of enslaved Africans) for the 150–175 vessels they had in the trade. Almost a quarter of all blacks living in the British empire in the late eighteenth century lived on the single island of Jamaica, to which, overall, a million Africans were shipped, and such was the death rate there (between one-fourth and one-half of all newly landed slaves died within three years) that it took the importation of half a million Africans to increase the island's slave population by a quarter of a million. We now know that of the ninety-six thousand slaves imported to the Chesapeake, all but 7 percent of them came directly from Africa.

There is a host of such numerical data in the essays on the Du Bois database. Numbers, simple quantities, matter. Magnitudes can make all the difference in our understanding. The accurate recording of them corrects false assumptions, establishes realistic parameters, and sets some of the basic terms of comprehension as one seeks to grasp the meaning of the greatest demographic phenomenon in Atlantic history before the migration of fifty million Europeans to the United States in the nineteenth and early twentieth centuries.

But striking, informative, and challenging as the numbers in themselves are, they do not explain themselves and are not in the end the goal of inquiry. For, as Lorena Walsh writes, "numbers alone, however refined, tell us little about cultural transfer, transformation, or annihilation among forcibly transplanted Africans."[1] Again and again the numbers provoke questions, new and important questions, that lead the authors to slip away from the quantitative data and probe for answers in the deep realms of social and cultural experience. Not all the questions the numbers raise can be answered: some explanations are reasonable inferences, some are informed guesses, some turn out to be simply discussions of the range of possible answers.

The most persistent explanatory theme that emerges from the data is the importance of ethnic and regional differences among the African people and the effect of these differences on all aspects of the process of enslavement, the demographic transfers, and the resulting Euro-African-American world in the Western Hemisphere.

David Eltis is the master technician, the most deeply versed in the statistical details of the database, but his figures lead him into speculative explanations of why, over 350 years, the "center of gravity of the Atlantic slave trade moved slowly north away from West Central Africa." Perhaps it was "the time, resources, and adjustment of social structures required to establish a supply network or to break through to new sources in the interior." "The distribution of Africans in the New World," he finds, "was no more random than the distribution of Europeans." Why? Was it determined by African ethnicity? African agency, he concludes, shaped the trade far more than we had suspected.[2]

Others resume the discussion in very specific ways. G. Ugo Nwokeji finds that to understand the structure of the African slave trade one must understand African conceptions of gender, and he demonstrates this in an elaborate discussion of the regionally differentiated roles of women in African economic, social, and military life. "Interregional differences in the gender division of labor" in Africa, he concludes, help explain the variant sex ratios in the slave trade. Specifically he shows how demographic changes in Africa resulted in the decline in the number of female slaves from Biafra.[3]

David Richardson, analyzing slave revolts, which he meticulously quantifies, considers all manner of shaping circumstances but remains puzzled as to why ships that had more than the normal proportion of slave women were more likely to have rebellions, and searches for an explanation in regional differences between slaves who did and those who did not revolt. He suspects that they largely derive from forces in Africa—the different regional and ethnic cultures and the timing and location of breakdowns in political order. But none of this is certain. Ahead, he writes, lies "a major research agenda" to uncover the complex "inter- and intraregional variations" that underlay the Africans' rebellions. One thing is definite: only an "African-centered explanation" will suffice.[4]

A parallel discussion follows from the database's statistics on transoceanic mortality. "Variations in the internal conditions in Africa," Herbert Klein and his collaborators write, "had a marked, direct impact on mortality." The most effective statistical discriminant in mortality rates is the Africans' ports of departure. Why? The patterns are puzzling. The domestic backgrounds must explain the differences. "More detailed study of patterns of variations" is needed.[5]

And for both David Geggus and Lorena Walsh, differentiated African cultures are the heart of the matter. The African roots of Haitian culture are no new theme, but in Geggus's paper it is part of an array of cultural patterns on Saint-Domingue—those of "Congos," West Central Africans, Igbos, and the Ewe-Fon people. For him, as for the other authors, there is no blur of undifferentiated "Africans." For all, it seems, the numbers require explanations in terms of highly specified African ethnicities, languages, and behavior patterns—ethnicity alone, in Walsh's article, being the key to the creation of new African-American identities. The Chesapeake, her figures show, was no "bewildering mix of African peoples . . . isolated from one another by a 'Babel of languages.'" She knows precisely where the Chesapeake slaves came from, how and why they were distributed among the riverine districts of Virginia and Maryland, and something of the consequences of those patterns of distribution in terms of creolization, family and gender structures, languages, and spiritual life.[6]

Even Stephen Behrendt, in his intricate explanation of the details of the complex marketing system in the Atlantic slave trade—a wonderful example of the functional integration of elements of the Atlantic world—finds that his firm numbers, which provide a lucid explanation of "transaction cycles on three continents," lead him into the less precise area of African agriculture, African trading patterns, and African entrepreneurship. And Trevor Burnard and Kenneth Morgan's paper on the marketing of slaves in Jamaica too, though based on rigorous statistical analysis, involves "heterogeneity of ethnic origins," the peculiar value placed on "men-boys and girls, none exceeding 16 or 18 years old," and a discussion of planters' preferences for people from specific African regions, based on assumptions of cultural characteristics.[7]

But if the sheer force of numbers and the importance of African agency in all aspects of the slave trade strike one forcibly, so too does a more subtle element, identified in Ralph Austen's essay. Obviously, the slave trade was a business, and a very profitable business, based on the commodification of human beings. One knows this to begin with, and one assumes at the start that we are dealing with a brutal, inhuman, devastating, tragic traffic that violates every shred of human sensibility. Even so, prepared as one is, as one reads these papers one recoils at the clinical, numerically accurate analysis of the trade—at the London merchant's reference to the salability of "small slaves and even Mangie Ones," at the reference to the "added value" of slaves by "seasoning" (sympathizing with the authors' sense of "the grotesqueness of the notion"), at the merchants' and planters' routine calculations of anticipated death rates, at the tricky supply problem of timber for "platforms" and iron for shackles, and at the normality of deaths in passage as a consequence of insurrection.

Informed as never before about the details of the slave trade, we can approach the subject objectively, impersonally, but only up to a point, beyond which we find ourselves emotionally involved. The whole story is still within living memory, and not only for people of African descent. We are all in some degree morally involved and must consider the relationship of history and memory.[8]

That problematic relationship has until recently been discussed mainly in connection with another global catastrophe, the Holocaust, in which six million Jews were deliberately killed. It was the tormenting recollection of that disaster, still part of living memory, that led to the founding of a journal, *History and Memory*, edited in Israel, in which the subject is constantly analyzed. But the problem's fullest theoretical exploration has appeared in France, in Pierre Nora's seven-volume *Lieux de mémoire*—sites of memory—of which a three-volume selection has appeared in English translation. Like so much of French methodological rumination, Nora's lengthy theoretical introductions and prefatory essays come across as rhetorical exuberance. But he has made the issue clear, and that issue lies at the latent foundation of the discussions of the slave trade.

History—that is, historiography—Nora explains, is the critical, skeptical, empirical source-bound reconstruction of past events, circumstances, and people based on the belief that the past is not only distant from us but also different. Historians look for differences in the past and for how those differences changed and evolved to create the world we know, which contains, however deeply buried, the residues of those past worlds. We avoid anachronisms of all kinds and seek to reconstruct the contexts of the past, the long-gone temporal and situational sockets in which past events and circumstances were embedded. As historians we shrink from telescoping past and present, hoping to explain the things that happened for their own sakes and in their own terms. And we select from the documentation what seems to illuminate the outcomes, which we, as opposed to the people in the past, are privileged to know. But we do so critically, skeptically, because we know that we can never recapture any part of the past absolutely and completely. So we keep our distance from the past, from the stories we tell, knowing that facts may be uncovered that will change our stories. Other view-points may turn us away from what we now think is relevant, and other ways of understanding may make us reconsider everything.

But memory, as Nora and others have explained, is something different. Its relation to the past is an embrace. It is not a critical, skeptical reconstruction of what happened. It is the spontaneous, unquestioned experience of the past. It is absolute, not tentative or distant, and it is expressed in signs and signals, symbols, images, and mnemonic clues of all sorts. It shapes our awareness whether we know it or not, and it is ultimately emotional, not intellectual.

Nora's project was based on his fear that France's memory of itself was fading, in part, he felt, because of the French historians' success in reducing the history of France to a critical contextualism in which no living memory can survive. So he set out to revive all those sites of memory, those *lieux de mémoire*, that contain and evoke the living, though fading, collective memory of the French people. Assembling a large team of historians, he and they wrote, and he published, short essays on everything he and they could think of as vital sites of French memory: Joan of Arc, the Eiffel Tower, Bastille Day, the Louvre, Verdun, the Protestant minority, the Tour de France, the genius of the French language, and so on, all this by way of bringing forward into current consciousness the cumulative, collective memory—not the history as a tentative reconstruction—of the French people.

There is obviously a history of the Atlantic slave trade and the African diaspora, and the new database and these highly professional papers have greatly improved that story. The now publicly available online database will be a permanent source for the future enrichment of our critical, contextual understanding of that long-gone phenomenon. But the memory of the slave trade is not distant; it cannot be reduced to an alien context; and it is not a critical, rational reconstruction. It is for us, in this society, a living and immediate, if vicarious, moral experience. It is buried in our consciousness and shapes our view of the world. Its sites, its symbols, its clues lie all about us. It is the Middle Passage that every child reads about in textbooks. It is evoked in novels and films that are less history than memory. It is what troubles us so deeply about Jefferson and Monticello. It lies barely below the surface in every discussion of race relations in public policy.

All of this, I believe, is not history, as we professionally practice it, but collective memory. As such it is inescapable for all of us, white or black, and we cannot distance ourselves from it by the rational reconstruction of the past. The history of the slave trade is a critically assembled, intellectually grasped story of distant events, but the memory of it is immediately urgent, emotional, and unconstrained by the critical apparatus of scholarship.

The deepest problem presented by the database, it seems to me, is how to understand the Atlantic slave trade as both history and memory. Gorée Island, off Senegal, as Ralph Austen explains, with its appalling holding pens, in fact "played a statistically minor part in this [slave] traffic," but it evokes the overwhelming memory of the entire human catastrophe with all its moral implications.[9]

Perhaps history and memory in the end may act usefully upon each other. The one may usefully constrain and yet vivify the other. The passionate, timeless memory of the slave trade that tears at our conscience and shocks our sense of decency may be shaped, focused, and informed by the critical history we write, while the history we so carefully compose may be kept alive, made vivid and constantly relevant and urgent by the living memory we have of it. We cannot afford to lose or diminish either if we are to understand who we are and how we got to be the way we are.

2

Context in History

It is no new thing to note the intersections between Australian and American history: the parallels and significant contrasts. Both countries—originally British settler societies imposed on aboriginal peoples whose worlds they destroyed—built their early economies on the labor of unfree people, though the consequences have been vastly different; both have struggled to throw off the confinements of provincialism in order to create their own identities, though the degree of success has differed; and though both are now multicultural nations, both are British institutionally and Anglophone culturally, a fact they respond to differently. But to see these familiar parallels and contrasts through the eyes and experiences of Charles Joseph La Trobe is to add a deeper dimension to the story.

For the man whose fate it would be to govern, or administer, both Victoria and Van Diemen's Land—then unformed, raucous, and rambunctious Anglo-frontier societies—had spent two years, 1832–33, traveling in America before he set foot in Australia. His account of that experience, the two-volume *The Rambler in North America*—which in some complicated way undoubtedly refracted the views of the strangely assorted pair he traveled with: the Swiss count Albert de Pourtalès and the American writer Washington Irving—is remarkably perceptive. La Trobe was described by Irving as "a man of a thousand occupations; a botanist, a geologist, a hunter of beetles and butterflies, a musical amateur, and sketcher of no mean pretensions; in short, a complete virtuoso";[1] and his virtuosity comes out clearly in the breadth of his interests in and the acuity of some of his observations on the North American scene he witnessed.

One startles at some of his comments, as at his wonderful observation that the locusts and other insects in North America sing in the key of C-sharp. Some of his perceptions are troubled and uncertain. He, like his Methodist kin, was a radical abolitionist, but he confessed that he could see only two eventualities for the slave society of the American Deep South: either the growing black population would in time "eat the white out of house and home" and take over the area most compatible to them, or a mulatto race would emerge "claiming an equality of rights and consideration." But his broadest generalizations are more confident and striking. The American people, La Trobe wrote,

are separated from the Old World by the vast ocean, but they are not without the influence of the vortex; every thing, their language, literature, necessities, increasing facility of communication with Europe, all render them intimately connected with us. We whirl, they whirl too. . . . [T]here may be this difference, that as yet they have more room, the sweep is a wider one than our's, but they still obey the same law as ourselves.

No one, La Trobe concluded, who travels through the United States from east to west and from north to south can fail to come away with the impression "that if on any part of His earthly creation, the finger of God has drawn characters which would seem to indicate the seat of empire—surely it is there!"[2]

Australia, he soon found, was different—different but yet similar to what he had discovered in North America, and it would be a project of some interest to examine that ambiguous relationship through La Trobe's eyes: to explore, through the many letters, official and personal, that he wrote in Australia and after,[3] something of the global diaspora of British culture and its creative encounters with two quite different environments.[4] To do that would not be easy, if only because of the difficulty of remaining faithful to the context of the time—the difficulty, that is, of resisting the compelling, almost irresistible tendency to select from the data of La Trobe's era anticipations of what we know eventuated in the later efflorescence and the subsequent decline of Britain's cultural empire.

And that—the problem of contextualism—is the issue I would like to comment on in what follows.

I am not concerned with anything abstract, with anything that might be called a philosophy of history, nor with such fashionable topics as history as fiction or any of the postmodern theories. I am concerned with one of the central problems in the everyday practice of history that contemporary historians actually face, none of whom, as far as I know, believe naively that historians can attain perfect objectivity; none of whom dream that a historian can contemplate the past from some immaculate cosmic perch, free from the prejudices, assumptions, and biases of one's own time, place, and personality; none of whom deny that facts are inert and meaningless until mobilized by an inquiring mind, and hence that all knowledge of the past is interpretative knowledge; yet all of whom assume that the reality of the past can be subjected to useful inquiries, that among the responses to those inquiries some views can be shown to be more accurate depictions of what actually happened than others, and that the establishment, in some significant degree, of a realistic understanding of the past, free of myths, wish-fulfillments, and partisan delusions, is essential for social sanity. They know that history, never a science, sometimes an art, is essentially a craft, and they try to improve their craftsmanship, knowing that they will never achieve anything like perfection, that in fact the inescapable limitations in what they can do will confine their work to approximations of what they seek, but that to despair for want of realizing the ideal would be to forfeit the mission which they are equipped to fulfill.

It is one of the central problems in the contemporary practice of history, faced by those who actually study the sources and attempt to reach conclusions and interpretations as close as possible to the actuality of what happened, that I would like to consider. It is the problem of recovering the contexts in which events take place: the settings, the unspoken assumptions, the perceptual universes of the participants which shape the meaning of events for those who experience them. The past is a different world, and we seek to understand it as it actually was. In a very loose sense, of course, one can say that all historical study is the search for past contexts since historians always try to reach deeply into the circumstances of the past. But the present effort to penetrate into the substructures of thought and behavior, into the silent assumptions, the perceptual maps, the interior experiences that shape overt expressions and events goes beyond the boundaries of traditional historical study—and it is full of problems.

At the simplest level, the difficulties of reaching back and locating events in their context are obvious. We cannot divest ourselves of our own assumptions, attitudes, beliefs, and experiences—strip away everything that intervened between then and now—in order to appreciate fully, identify with that other, distant way of thinking, feeling, and behaving. We cannot experience what they experienced in the way they experienced it. We cannot contract our expanded sense of possibilities into their more limited sphere, nor project our skepticism into their sense of wonder and belief. And we can have little notion of what were commonplaces to them, underlying but shaping circumstances so ordinary and unremarkable as to have been subliminal—everyday discomforts (of clothing that itched, of shoes that tore the feet, of lice, fleas, and vermin); the ubiquity of filth in public places; the constant sound of urban bells in medieval Europe; the automatic, unthinking management of personal hygiene; the constant expectation of incomprehensible illnesses and sudden death; the sense of the reality, urgency, and plenitude of animist forces; the absence or scarcity of print; the slow pace of communication and travel; the assumption of utterly unbridgeable social distances, distances so great as to stimulate awe, not envy. All of those ordinary circumstances of life are almost completely unrecoverable precisely because they were so ordinary, so unremarkable hence unremarked.

And beyond that there is another obvious difficulty in recovering the contexts of the past. The fact—the inescapable fact—is that we know how it all came out, and they did not. No more by them then than by us now could the future be imagined. The natural orientation of their experience was to their past. Our perspective, in studying their lives, is formed by what proved to be their future, which is our past, the ignorance of which was the most profound circumstance of their lives. We will never fully recapture their uncertainty and re-create it in the fabric of the history we write.

The inner logic of what we do leads us in the opposite direction. Knowing the outcome, we feel it to be our obligation to show the process by which the known eventuality came about. So we try to describe the path from then to now, and in doing so select for our accounts the elements in a once indeterminate situation that appear to have led to the future outcome. Our histories will therefore attempt to make clear, if not the inevitability of what happened, at least the logic of why it happened as it did, and so it seems that we have no reason to dwell on initial uncertainties, or to attempt to recover the original ambiguities and make them real.

It is this aspect of the difficulties inherent in the effort to recover past contexts that leads me back to that still remarkable little book of Herbert Butterfield, *The Whig Interpretation of History*. Most historians know that slim volume of 1931, but it is worth recalling in this connection. In it, Butterfield probed the core problems of contextualism more deeply than anyone had done before. He was, in fact, the first historian to attempt a formulation of the issues and to point out the dangers and values involved. And while his book and his later writing on the subject, which continued throughout his career, were first attacked, then taken for granted, his classic statement of 1931 set out the terms of discussion—so successfully, indeed, that some have said that it "effectively blocked further discussion and debate."[5]

Butterfield's aim in that resonant book (it is, as I will indicate, still the subject of controversy) was simply to show the inevitable falsification of history—what he called the "gigantic optical illusion"—that results from studying the past with reference to the present, and the irresistible "magnet for ever pulling at our minds" that leads us to extract from complex, ambiguous contexts of the past the seeds of future outcomes. The Whig historians of the nineteenth century particularly, Butterfield argued so famously, seeking the roots of modern progressive liberalism, which they approved of, selected, in describing critical turning points, what appeared to be the antecedents, the early, struggling origins of our present world, and celebrated these nascent impulses. So Luther and the Protestant Reformation had been described as the harbingers of religious toleration, and the Reform Bill of 1832 a massive impetus to parliamentary democracy. But in fact, Butterfield pointed out, Luther was no more in favor of religious toleration than was the pope; the supporters of the Reform Bill had no interest in universal male suffrage or votes for women, and defended the profitable abuses of politics as strongly as their opponents. Parliamentary democracy, like religious toleration, arose gradually, Butterfield wrote, from complex interactions of ambiguous and even internally contradictory forces in which good and evil, right and wrong existed on all sides.

But such whiggish foreshortenings and anachronisms, Butterfield argued, which increase radically the more history is abridged, are not the exclusive property of the nineteenth-century Whigs. They result, he wrote, from "a trick of organization, an unexamined habit of mind that any historian may fall into," which is the product of the simplification of the ambiguities and contradictions inherent in all historical contexts: the naive praise for those who seem to have favored the development of the future and blame for those who apparently tried to block it, the equally naive assumption that consequences result from intentions, and above all, the orientation of history to the future of the past—that is, to the historian's present—rather than to the past's own past. The chaos, the rich ambiguity of historical moments, life's bafflements, the accidents and contingencies—all of that, Butterfield believed, must be retained if history is to be a true account of human experience. And beyond all of that lies that "most useless and unproductive of all forms of reflection: the dispensing of moral judgments upon people or upon actions in retrospect"—heroism and villainy, good and evil being most often designations imposed by the winners.[6]

In his own historical writing Butterfield tried to be as good as his word, and consistently carried over his doctrine of moral neutrality—based on his personal belief that only God can truly judge—to public commentaries on what he took to be the moral ambiguities of the Cold War. This earned him abuse from both liberals and conservatives, hawks and doves, in Cold War politics.[7] Of his main substantive works of history, one, *The Origins of Modern Science,* originally a series of lectures, is a popular survey, an abridgement, that illustrates with remarkable clarity his hopes for history that is truly contextual. "The whole fabric of our history of science," he wrote,

> is lifeless and its whole shape is distorted if we seize upon this particular man in the fif-

teenth century who had an idea that strikes us as modern, now upon another man of the sixteenth century who had a hunch or an anticipation of some later theory. . . . It has proved almost more useful to learn something of the misfires and the mistaken hypotheses of early scientists, to examine the particular intellectual hurdles that seemed insurmountable at given periods, and even to pursue courses of scientific development which ran into a blind alley, but which still had their effect on the progress of science in general. . . . It is not sufficient to read Galileo with the eyes of the twentieth century or to interpret him in modern terms—we can only understand his work if we know something of the system which he was attacking, and we must know something of that system apart from the things which were said about it by its enemies.

So in discussing Copernicus, Butterfield stressed the degree to which his theory "was only a modified form of the Ptolemaic system"; it simplified but retained the then current doctrines of spheres and epicycles, and, further, Copernicus's teachings were enmeshed in "teleological explanations and forms of what we should call animism." So William Harvey, Butterfield wrote, while demonstrating *de novo* the circulation of the blood, remained in many ways an Aristotelian, and believed in vital spirits. And Newton was intensely concerned with apocalyptic prophecies and was immersed in alchemical studies.[8]

Butterfield's *The Origins of Modern Science*—whose themes historians of science of far greater technical knowledge than Butterfield's would develop, qualify, and criticize[9]—is only an elementary general survey, but it is just the kind of abridgement he thought most likely to suffer from anachronistic distortion. Yet when his hoped-for contextualism appears in densely researched and fully elaborated writing, in mature works of historical scholarship, it has about it an exceptional ring of truth.

So too does Frances Yates's *The Rosicrucian Enlightenment,* despite the criticism it has received. It is a brilliant excavation of an intellectual and cultural world that seemed, to the few modern historians before her who were aware of it, so regressive, bizarre, and ephemeral that they generally ignored it. But Yates managed to show, by dint of profound research in esoteric writings, in prints crowded with symbolic meanings, and in the subtle resonances of words and phrases, that the mingled hermeticism, cabalism, mysticism, and alchemical lore of sixteenth- and early-seventeenth-century Rosicrucianism formed a true movement for the enlightened reform of mankind. For all its obscurities, it had links, however indirect, to the founding of the Royal Society and constituted one of the stages by which Renaissance learning evolved into the Enlightenment of the eighteenth century. "Like archaeologists," Yates wrote, "digging down through layers, we have found under the superficial history of the early seventeenth century . . . a whole culture, a whole civilization, lost to view, and not the less important because of such a short duration." By the eighteenth century, Rosicrucianism, which in its origins had sought to advance learning, ameliorate human suffering, and introduce a new era of universal brotherhood and goodwill, was dismissed as hopelessly archaic and obscurantist—the opposite of enlightened; but Yates showed that in the true context of its origins it was the first step in the progress of reform.[10]

Similarly, Keith Thomas in his *Religion and the Decline of Magic* showed the vital intermingling, in late medieval and early modern times, of ancient magical practices with revealed religion. His account of the inextricable intertwining of magical beliefs and practices with Christianity is so persuasive that in the end, after 650 pages, he himself is left to wonder, as are his readers, how people ever managed to extract themselves from this complex entanglement. Yes, Thomas wrote, "magic was ceasing to be intellectually acceptable" in the seventeenth century; and yes, "religion taught them to try self help before invoking supernatural aid." But we are "forced to the conclusion that men emancipated themselves from these magical beliefs without necessarily having devised any effective technology with which to replace them," and so, he concluded, "the ultimate origins of this faith in unaided human capacity remain mysterious."[11]

Is it not true that the authentic contexts of origins are full of complexities and uncertainties, confusions and dead ends, which Whiggish "clarifications" will necessarily ignore or distort? Thus, in a different sphere, one of the key documents in the origins of Freud's thought and of the psychoanalytic movement is Freud's correspondence with Wilhelm Fliess. They were both part of a great stirring of thought, an explosion of creative experimentation and unfettered theorizing about interior states of being and about the human personality, that took off in all directions in the late nineteenth century and that had no certain outcome and many dead ends. An informed contemporary in the 1890s, reading the Freud/Fliess correspondence, might well have criticized both for their strange notions. Both, in the creative ferment of the time, believed they had discovered the sexual roots of emotional disturbances, but they followed different paths. Fliess had one theory, Freud had another. Fliess concluded from his studies that the physiological seat of sexuality lay in the nose, and that there was a twenty-three-day cycle in male sexuality that bore some relation to astronomical movements. Freud believed that he had found something important in infantile sexuality, in tales of childhood seductions, and in the relation of dreams to psychoneurotic symptoms. The medical profession and the public at large paid little more attention to Freud's *Interpretation of Dreams,* which proved to be seminal, than it did to Fliess's monograph on the relationship between the nose and the female sexual organs, which did not. In context, both works were expressions of a wave of fresh, groping experimental thinking which in retrospect one can see liberated Freud's mind to find its way into a deeper understanding than had been known before. But for an important period in his early career Freud wondered whether Fliess had gotten it right, and he showed the utmost courtesy to the ideas of his imaginative colleague.[12]

There are other striking examples of sustained efforts to recover lost contexts—the confused, uncertain ambiences from which developments that shaped the future emerged; but they are rare. Robert Darnton has relentlessly pursued not the well-known master writings of the Enlightenment and their effect on reform and revolution, nor reform or revolution as such, but "the structure of the cultural world under the Old Regime"[13]—the Grub Street scribblings, the popular publications catering to ordinary taste, even the pornography of the eighteenth century, all of which nourished the deeper, innately rebellious cultural context from which more formal antiestablishment thinking developed and which would later erupt in the Jacobin upheaval.

Quentin Skinner, in his search for "meaning and understanding in the history of ideas," has produced finely wrought essays that circle around the problem of context in interpreting ideas. While he explicitly rejects the reductionist contextualism "of religious, political, and economic factors" as the determinants of the meaning of a text, he bases his approach, in his two-volume *Foundations of Modern Political Thought* and in his many essays, on the necessity "to situate the text in its linguistic or ideological context: [that is,] the collection of texts written or used in the same period, addressed to the same or similar issues and sharing a number of conventions." Skinner is in fact a radical contextualist, to the dismay of other intellectual historians, like John Patrick Diggins, who fear that the transhistorical meanings of ideas, their transcendent validity and timeless authority, will be destroyed if they are hobbled by contextual limitations. The monograph series Skinner coedited is called *Ideas in Context.* The anthology of his essays and those of his leading critics is entitled *Meaning and Context,* And while he deprecates some of Butterfield's arguments, he pleads, just as Butterfield did, for "strict historicity" and agrees with Butterfield's central position, which in Skinner's terms becomes the insistence that the key to recovering the historical meaning of a text lies in limiting attention to the surrounding texts that "the author might himself have avowed" and "in recovering the complex intentions of the author in writing it."[14]

The effort to understand manifest events and crucial texts by locating them in their original context has many expressions. Among them are the extensive writings on the ideological setting of the American Revolution, which spill over into the recent outpouring on republicanism and liberalism, on the American Founders' "original intent," and on the rights and wrongs of the Revolutionaries' interpretation of the British constitution.[15]

That vast interpretative campaign, with its ramifications in contemporary constitutional, legal, and political controversies, began as an effort to locate not the famous, formal, abstract principles of the American Revolution or of the American Enlightenment, but the deeper context: the configuration of fears, beliefs, and aspirations that underlay those manifest principles and that fundamentally shaped the world view of the American leaders. These leaders were not a disengaged intelligentsia. They were not rigorous thinkers—philosophers, political scientists, or theorists of any kind. They were lawyers, preachers, planters, farmers, and merchants immersed in their own business, and part-time provincial politicians. The problem of interpretation was to reconstruct the underlying view of the public world that these people derived from scattered readings, pulpit preachings, their own political experience, and the information that reached them through the Atlantic communication network. In time that eighteenth-century ideology was reconstructed. It was shown to have been derived from a broad array of sources but given distinctive shape by the arguments and polemics of the opposition publicists and politicians in Britain, and the public moralists, whose efforts at political reform had failed in the home country. It was shown, in addition, how the inner workings of these underlying ideas, fears, and beliefs, deeply embedded in the peculiarities of eighteenth-century Anglo-American life and culture, came to constitute triggers of political and military action under certain conditions.[16]

This was a contextual reading that interpreted the Revolutionaries' thinking as a product of their own peculiar history, intellectual as well as political, and of the limited conditions of their own time. It quickly came under attack by those who demanded more immediate relevance to the modern world. Some assumed that all revolutions must have roots in social and economic crises; for them, this was a hopelessly "idealist" interpretation that must have more to do with rhetoric than with reality. Others, willing to concede that an eighteenth-century revolution need not conform to post-Marxian prescriptions, felt that it was *not sufficiently* intellectualized—it must be associated with, and be seen to derive from, a deeper, more systematic, pan-European ideological movement which scholars had recently described as "civic humanism." This was a phrase unknown to eighteenth-century Americans, but which these historians found to be a convenient predecessor and foil for the presumed advent in the early nineteenth century of its opposite, "liberalism"—that is, possessive individualism and competitive capitalism—which the humanist Founders, these historians said, would have condemned. Still others refused to believe that sensible Americans could have derived from their world view a conviction that they were faced with a conspiracy at the heart of the British government, a "design" to deprive them of their liberties, despite the fact that the Revolutionary leaders said exactly that time after time, wrote it into the Declaration of Independence, and explained the reality of that danger in cogent historical, logical, and political terms. To take that fear seriously in view of what we now know of the bumbling inefficiency of the British government, it was said, would be to dismiss the Founding Fathers as paranoids. But given what in fact these eighteenth-century provincials knew of their own and Britain's recent history and politics, the turmoils and conspiracies the liberal establishment had survived in living memory, and the fragility and recency of constitutional protections, they were sensible and realistic indeed. And they were as much capitalist "liberals" as they were communitarian humanists. To make their ideas, and the Revolutionary movement generally, conform to later prescriptions, to more formal doctrines, or to twentieth-century sensibilities and notions of reality is to distort the character of that distant world and create one of Butterfield's "optical illusions" which blind us to the peculiarities and ambiguities of the past.

The difficulty of recovering the context in this case, and of keeping it free from anachronistic distortions, is typical of the problems one faces at this level of historical interpretation. Such difficulties can to some extent, however, be overcome—by the amassment of detailed knowledge of the past; by the skill that can be developed in piecing documentary fragments together into strange but meaningful mosaics; by close attention to the losers (Butterfield's misfires and blind alleys); and by the constant effort to imagine the distinctiveness of distant worlds. And there have been notable successes in recovering at least some of the subtlest, most interior experiences of people in the past, experiences that are strikingly different from our own.

But to the extent that one succeeds in this kind of historical archaeology, one confronts consequences that raise difficult problems that have ignited bitter contention in contemporary politics.

The first problematic consequence of succeeding in contextualizing history is essentially moral. To explain contextually is, implicitly at least, to excuse.

One could explain, with reference to the context of the time, the logical reasons why the American Constitution did not eliminate slavery. But it seems to be moral obtuseness to say that the framers of the Constitution had good reasons for what they did. However understandable these reasons may have been, to try to explain them seems to be an attempt to excuse them, while what historians should be doing, according to some, is condemning them and focusing on the immorality of slavery and the Founders' moral blinders.

Jefferson was a liberal, imaginative, and sensitive man, and he sincerely loathed slavery; he called it "an abominable crime" and a blot on civilization. Then why did he not free his slaves? Consistent with the Revolution's egalitarianism, there was a short-lived abolitionist movement in the 1780s; surely it should have been advanced and exploited by people like Jefferson. But it was not. And the seeming dilemma is not resolved by noting that though Jefferson's generation did not rid the country of slavery they did a great deal to restrict it. They scheduled the slave trade for extinction and prohibited slavery itself in what would become the five states of the Old Northwest, while the northeastern states set in motion legal processes that would abolish it. Above all, the Revolution made of slavery a problem it had never been before. Before the Revolution, slavery was rarely seen as a problem; after the Revolution, there never was a time when slavery was not a problem.

All of that transformed the whole issue of slavery. But in view of that, the question, it seems, becomes even more insistent: If they came so close to eliminating slavery completely, why did they stop where they did? It does not seem good enough to say that the people who wrote the Constitution were more interested in creating and sustaining the fragile Union than in running the risk of destroying it over the issue of slavery. To suggest that they knew what they were talking about is somehow to exonerate the evil of slavery: it is morally obtuse.

This is no casual matter. The attacks on Jefferson over the issue of slavery have escalated astonishingly in recent years, and have overwhelmed him and the other American Founders—hence in a sense the foundations of the American nation—with charges not only of racism but of blatant hypocrisy. So Michael Zuckerman finds that the only explanation of Jefferson's refusal, as president, to come to the aid of the revolution in Saint-Domingue (Haiti) lay in "his antipathy to black autonomy." Jefferson and his partisans, Zuckerman writes, could not see beyond their racist scorn for the Haitian revolutionaries and the threat they seemed to pose for white society everywhere. Jefferson, Zuckerman writes, "was a man intellectually undone by his negrophobia . . . he was ultimately prepared to abandon all else in which he believed—and believed passionately—sooner than surrender his racial repugnances." No amount of contextual explanation will excuse his behavior, for Jefferson, Zuckerman concludes—going to the heart of the issue—"was not as confined by his culture as his apologists have often claimed. . . . [H]e was certainly not simply a sufferer of the constraints of his situation." And Michael Lind, in a furious assault, calls Jefferson "the greatest southern reactionary," whose tradition naturally and logically culminates in the careers of Theodore Bilbo and Strom Thurmond. "Jefferson was obsessed, in particular, by the fear that his precious Anglo-Saxon nation would be corrupted by intermarriage with nonwhites. . . . Every major feature of the modern United States—from racial equality to Social Security, from the Pentagon to the suburb—represents a repudiation of Jeffersonianism."[17]

To suggest that Jefferson and his generation of Anglo-American reformers—radical but pragmatic idealists whose reforms transformed the world—were confronting without precedent or guidance the problem of racial differences in a theoretically egalitarian society, and that they were struggling with the related dilemma of bondage, an immemorial condition, in a free society, evokes Zuckerman's bitterest condemnation. The fact that as he aged Jefferson sought increasingly to throw off the racist assumptions he had inherited, writing only six years after the Haitian crisis that blacks "are gaining daily in the opinions of nations, and hopeful advances are making towards their re-establishment on an equal footing with the other colors of the human family"—all of that pales next to what Zuckerman and others consider to have been Jefferson's "negrophobia."

The moral issue inherent in contextual history seems inescapable. Even Butterfield at one point felt obliged to reconsider the central arguments in his *The Whig Interpretation* and transpose them to a different plane. In 1938, lecturing in Nazi Germany on the history of historical writing, he made what appeared to be a sharp reversal. "The whig interpretation," he told the Germans, "which in my view had long been a barrier to historical understanding turned out to have been at one time the initial stage in a general advance . . . an important factor in the development not merely of whigs but of the whole political tradition—indeed the political consciousness—of Englishmen." Whig history was still bad history, but Butterfield realized during the crisis of the war years that it had had the benevolent effect of enshrining political liberty in the nation's consciousness and creating a stabilizing sense of historical continuity in the development of the British constitution. The book that Butterfield developed from those lectures, *The Englishman and His History,* published during the war, is a celebration of the triumph of England's political achievements that would have warmed the hearts not only of Macaulay and the Trevelyans but of that quintessential moralist Lord Acton.[18]

But the moral issue of contextual history is perhaps most fully and deeply revealed in another area—in the bitter polemics of Irish historiography. These disputes, paralleling Ireland's political struggles, go back in their origins to earlier generations, but they continue with undiminished severity.

The traditional story of Irish history—the whig interpretation, as it would now be called—was that of a long struggle for national liberation, which dated back to the twelfth century, expressed in a series of bloody rebellions or uprisings against English oppressors which eventuated in the Proclamation of the

Republic by the rebels of 1916, and the creation of the Irish Free State in 1922.

Such was—and is—the standard nationalist view of Ireland's history. But in recent times there came a powerful wave of revisionist writing, deeply contextualist, whose goal, according to the Cambridge historian Brendan Bradshaw, was to expose "the nationalist epic . . . as an ideologically motivated myth." And the revisionists' mentor, Bradshaw writes, was none other than Herbert Butterfield. His arguments for a "value-free and 'past-centered' history," according to Bradshaw, became in Ireland a dismissal, a refutation of the traditional nationalist account. The story of Ireland's "historic liberation struggle" became so completely debunked as a myth that in 1986 the most prominent of the younger historians of Ireland, Roy Foster, could entitle a key programmatic statement, ostensibly conciliatory, "We Are All Revisionists Now."

He was wrong, according to Bradshaw, whose blasting rebuttal continues to center on Butterfield and the moral implications of his contextualist views. "The Olympian detachment" that Butterfield prescribed, Bradshaw writes, his

> "past-centered history" is morally objectionable as a retreat to the ivory tower and an abdication of the special public function of the historian: to promote social understand-

ing of how the community has got to where it is. . . . The great patriots, entered for veneration in the nationalist canon, emerged from the devil's advocacy of the revisionists as a rogues' gallery . . . of power-hungry megalomaniacs and nincompoops. More objectionably, the catastrophic dimension of Irish history—conquest, colonization, dispossession, religious and social discrimination, immiseration—was subjected to a process of normalisation and, indeed, tacit evasion, designed to rid Irish history of its legacy of bitterness.

Normalization by contextual analysis, which tends to rob the past of its moral qualities, is the heart of a technical problem—in Irish historiography as in any other. In context, the Ulster rising of 1641, traditionally understood as "the first of the great nationalist rebellions of the modern period, the first major attempt to throw off the yoke of British oppression," can now be seen to have begun, as Aidan Clarke put it, as a conservative "preservationist movement" by "members of the propertied class" who were loyal to the English crown and who did not "display that implacable hostility towards England which characterised the contemporary stereotype of 'the Irish.'" And even in its later, wilder phase, the rising of 1641 was, Clarke wrote, a momentary upheaval of "pre-modern, rural . . . kin-centred and backward-looking" people lacking "modern" concepts of nationality and confessional identity.

It would be difficult to exaggerate the bitterness of the debate, thus formulated, on Irish history. Symposia, argumentative reviews, charges and countercharges, and detailed monographs on both sides of the issue have been published year after year, and the conceptual focus continues to center on the moral implications of contextual history. I am not saying, Desmond Fennell of Dublin wrote, that historians *must* reconcile factual truth with "the pattern of meaning and moral interpretation" which their predecessors, their culture, their nation, have established. I *am* saying, Fennell declared, that historians who do combine a factual accuracy with moral judgments consistent with their nation's moral sense of itself

contribute to the well-being of the nation, and that those not so disposed . . . do not. Fortunate the nation whose historians are mainly of the former kind, unfortunate the nation in which historians of the latter kind predominate.[19]

There is nothing peculiarly Irish about this problem. A. J. P. Taylor's effort to reduce Hitler's foreign policy in the 1930s to the normal practices of pragmatic European expansionists in his *The Origins of the Second World War* (1961) created a furor that raged for years. It is a matter of context, not morality, Taylor wrote. Hitler

> aimed to make Germany the dominant Power in Europe and maybe, more remotely, in the world. Other Powers treat smaller countries as their satellites. Other Powers seek to defend their vital interests by force of arms. In international affairs there was nothing wrong with Hitler except that he was a German.

"I make no moral judgments of my own," Taylor insisted. "Who am I to say that [the Versailles Treaty] was 'moral' or 'immoral' in the abstract? From what point of view—that of the Germans, of the Allies, of neutrals, of the Bolsheviks? Some of its makers thought that it was moral; some thought it necessary; some thought it both immoral and unnecessary."[20]

Taylor's views could be disputed, and they have been, but they could not be ignored. He knew too much about the details of international relations to be ignored; he could too convincingly show the similarity of Hitler's opportunistic aggression in foreign affairs to that of the other European powers—just as others could show the similarity of the Hitlerjugend to Roosevelt's Civilian Conservation Corps;[21] and he was better able than most of his critics to mobilize a mass of information into a cogent argument.

The tendency to obscure the moral dimensions of history grows as the penetration into the details and subtleties of past contexts deepens and the extraordinary becomes normalized—within the situation of its time. It is a systematic, inherent problem, a seemingly inescapable consequence of this approach to history—but it is not the only one. Equally important and perplexing is the problem of dynamics—of explaining change, process, evanescence, which lie at the heart of historical understanding. The more deeply and fully one explains how things were, how things functioned, the more one loses control of the dynamics of change. For the disturbing elements, the disequilibrating forces, the motives for change, are necessarily subordinated in any situation one describes in depth, since it is the stable—that is, the dominant—elements that are most relevant to the effort at hand. If one gives a fully contextual picture of what was going on at a particular time, one will inevitably subordinate the disturbing elements, which lead to change, to the controlling, stable elements. Therefore how can one show why or how things changed? Why did the secondary forces become dominant? What events upset the situation?

There are vivid illustrations of this problem. I have already mentioned Keith Thomas's difficulty in explaining why deeply embedded, immemorial magical practices declined in the seventeenth century, why they ceased "to be intellectually acceptable." But it is in Australia that the problem of dynamics—of change and evanescence—in contextual history is most vividly illustrated. The eleven-volume Australian bicentennial history is one of the most elaborate efforts in contextual history ever written. Six of the volumes are reference works, but in the five core volumes the authors rejected narrative history altogether and concentrated on a series of deep probes—"slices"— at fifty-year intervals. It was in this form—as five volume-length "social portraits of Australia at arbitrarily chosen moments of the past": 1788, 1838, 1888, 1938, and from 1939—that these distinguished historians and anthropologists chose to tell Australia's national history.[22]

Why? Australia's history could not be properly understood, Graeme Davison explained, in standard narrative form—as a story—because, he wrote, narration involves a "linear conception of time," has an "inbuilt ideological bias," and allows only a "narrow selection of causal factors." Linear narration, Davison continued, in a freshly rethought and expanded version of Butterfield's early arguments, creates a mere illusion of causal links since the historian "selects those facts or events which appear to favour [the] known outcome and he ignores those which are irrelevant to it, whether or not they seemed important to contemporaries." Properly understood, causation involves the interplay of forces—economic, demographic, political, social, cultural—which can only be explained in the deep context of static "slices." Narration necessarily skates over the surface, while "slice" history "encourages us to examine functional relationships within a society" and it does not "preclude a recognition of conflict or change." For the traditional distinction between history and the social sciences—the former supposedly devoted to studying "causal links through time," the latter devoted to discovering "the 'social laws' prevailing within a particular society"—is now "of course," Davison wrote, "hopelessly outmoded." Sociologists, he explained, are now also concerned with questions of time and change; social historians do nothing different. Since, therefore, "the disciplinary barriers have come down," and since it is obvious that national narratives are only a "device by which historians create the illusion of a common purpose or destiny," deep contextual penetrations, spaced at selected intervals, can best convey the truth of a nation's past. For

> the slice approach acts as a corrective to the inbuilt teleological bias of narrative history.

It implies that we temporarily abstain from the search for "the most significant years, or the busiest or the epochal" and concentrate instead upon the routine, the ordinary and the mundane. Instead of assigning significance to events in terms of a known outcome or *telos* it gently subverts the "received notion of the rhythms or contours of Australian history." Instead of exalting the established heroes of Australian history, it aims to rescue the struggling selector, the suburban housewife, even perhaps the landboomer's clerk, from the "appalling condescension of posterity."[23]

The five "slice" volumes do indeed cover most aspects of Australian life in those years—everything that was going on in the politics, religion, culture, economy, society, climate, flora and fauna in the selected years, and many of the connections among these aspects of life. But the problem of dynamics remains. There is little indication of how or why Australia changed between 1788 and 1838 or between 1888 and 1938, and to the extent that such explanations can be found in these volumes, they in fact take the form of narratives—"linear" micronarratives inserted along the way. If readers of all 2,330 pages of the five volumes understand how modern Australia evolved—the process by which it has become what it is—it must be because they already know the nation's basic narrative history and can associate these five contextual probes with that story.

Such, it seems to me, are some of the problems and consequences that flow from the effort to penetrate beyond manifest events into their contextual settings, into the substructures and surroundings from which they emerge—the unspoken assumptions and latent conditions—and to recover the uncertainties, failures, ambiguities, and bafflements from which what were to become confident successes develop. The problems in this kind of history, in my view the deepest history, are difficult and subtle, and they create great demands on historians: to suspend their present commitments sufficiently to enter different worlds, to broaden their sympathies for people not only distant but alien from themselves, to respond sensitively to apparent anomalies that lead into unsuspected complexities, to distinguish consequences from intentions, and yet to do all that while retaining both the capacity for moral judgments that do not warp the narrative and the conviction that change, growth, decline—evanescence—is what history is all about.

I do not think history has collapsed into sociology or anthropology or some kind of ethnosocial science. We will always need to know, in some sequential—that is to say, narrative—form, what has happened in the past, what the struggles were all about, where we have come from; and we will always need to extend the poor reach of our own immediate experience into other lives, accurately portrayed, that have gone before. But we will do so in more complicated and sophisticated ways than we have in the past. History in the richest sense must be, I believe, what Butterfield said it should be, both a study and a story—that is, structural studies woven into narratives that explain the long-term process of change and the short-term accidents, decisions, and encounters which together changed the world from what it had been. But we must all still be storytellers, narrators—though of events lodged deep in their natural contexts.

3

Three Trends in Modern History

G ordon Wright, speaking from this rostrum a few years ago, warned that those who have the honor of perpetuating the American Historical Association's ritual of presidential addresses "might do well not to take their pronouncements as the voice of God or the crystallized wisdom of the ages," and he wondered if it were not significant that the president is allowed only one parting shot to speak *ex cathedra,* "not at the outset of his term of office but at the very end, only forty-eight hours before he 'passes into history,' as the saying goes. By that time it is much too late for him to make promises, to influence the Association's future course, or even to be held to answer for his steward-ship or for such sophistries as his swan song may con-tain." Having thus taken the curse off any *ex cathedra* pronouncements that might follow, he proceeded to pronounce on one of the most elevated, difficult, and controversial issues that faces historians who think about what they do—namely, the degree to which history is a moral science.[1] I admire his courage, but I take my lead from his warning. What follows is noth-ing more than the identification of and some preliminary thoughts on three animating trends as I see them emerging from recent historical writing—trends that are likely to shape any comprehensive narratives that reflect the knowledge and analytical skills we now have.

The first becomes clear through a consideration of the importance of quantification. Quantification in history is easily misunderstood. It is distinct from computation and the formal analysis made possible by computers. Further, as Oscar Handlin and others have shown, if it is not practiced with careful discrimination and by historians otherwise informed of historical reality, it can destroy the foundations of historical understanding by limiting questions to available numerical answers, by endowing with a spurious rigor claims that have no basis in fact, and by diverting attention from the central themes of an evolving inquiry.[2] But beyond all of that, the innovations that are claimed for quantification are exaggerated. Historians have always used numbers, when they could get them; they have always attempted to convey magnitudes in numerical as well as verbal terms. Yet there *is* something in the current development of quantification in history that is new and that will, I think, affect the future evolution of historical writing generally.

Some terms borrowed from Freud and the sociologists may help one see the character of this development. It is reasonable, I think, to say that almost all history written before the twentieth century was essentially *manifest* history. That is, history was the story of events that contemporaries were clearly aware of, that were matters of conscious concern, were consciously struggled over, were, so to speak, headline events in their own time even if their causes and their underlying determinants were buried below the level of contemporaries' understanding. And this could hardly have been otherwise. The available documentation was derived largely from public records, from the personal archives of men and women much involved in the headline events of their own time, and from literary accounts of other kinds variously focused on manifest events. Underlying circumstances, however skillfully and imaginatively described, were secondary concerns introduced as prefatory matter, or interleaved here and there to help explain the main events or to help create a realistic picture of the era in which the events took place. Sometimes these prefatory or contextual descriptions were effective, but however effective these passages may have been, they formed an accompaniment to, a commentary on, a background for the essential foreground, which remains the story of manifest events.

What is new, it seems to me, about the current work in quantitative history is not that numbers as such are being introduced, or more precise numbers than we have had before, but that the kind of numbers being introduced is making possible a new range of inquiry into what might be called *latent* events—that is, events that contemporaries were not fully or clearly aware of, at times were not aware of at all, events that they did not consciously struggle over, however much they might have been forced unwittingly to grapple with their consequences, and events that were not recorded as events in the documentation of the time. No one in the seventeenth-century Chesapeake colonies knew that population growth was slowing in Britain and that labor markets were shifting in ways that contracted the flow of white indentured servants to the colonies. The planters only knew that they found themselves relying more and more on the cost-effectiveness of slave labor. The latent history of population growth in seventeenth-century Britain was uncovered by twentieth-century students of population history using quantitative analysis, who also established the fact that it was only in the mid-1680s, and not before, that blacks formed the majority of the Chesapeake region's labor force.

Similarly, no one in the Tuscan countryside ravaged by the Black Death in the mid-fourteenth century associated that fearful manifestation of God's wrath with an earlier population decline that had been in motion for a century before the plague struck Europe. It was modern historians who uncovered this latent, long-term event, entered it, so to speak, into

the record, and associated it with the manifest devastation of the plague. This earlier decline could be
discovered only in statistics created out of the manuscript tax records and the great Florentine survey, the
Catasto, of 1427.

It is not simply that quantification is making possible a more precise description of these latent events.
The events I am referring to were known, if at all,
only vaguely by contemporaries or by previous historians to have *been* events. Taken together, they form
a new landscape, like that of the ocean floor, assumed
to have existed in some vague way by people struggling at the surface of the waves but never seen before
as actual rocks, ravines, and cliffs. And like the newly
discovered ocean floor the world of latent events can
be seen to be directly involved in the manifest history
of the surface world itself. And that is my point.

One of the most important developments in current historiography, it seems to me, is the emerging
integration of latent and manifest events. I do not
mean simply that a deeper picture of the context of
public events is appearing, although that is happening,
but that events of one order are being brought together
with events of another order. The resulting conflation
is beginning to produce the outline of a general history different from what we have known before.

Major public events will of course remain in their
key locations, but when seen in connection with the

clarifying latent landscape they appear to occupy rather different positions than heretofore. The American Revolution, for example, transformed American life and influenced the course of events elsewhere in the world. That manifest event will not be obscured by discoveries of events of another order, but explanations of the origins, development, and consequences of the Revolution are beginning to take on quite different forms in the light of latent events that are now being uncovered; events in the population and migration history of the pre-Revolutionary years, settlement patterns, and attitudes to authority, all of which helped shape the origins and outcome of the Revolution. How could the treatment of slavery have been uniform throughout the newly independent American states given the different balances of Creoles and Africans that we have recently discovered existed and given the different degrees and forms of assimilation that we now know developed and that have only recently been located with some precision on the chronological map of American history?

The integration of latent and manifest events was not planned. It was no one's "research design." It is emerging from the convergence of the efforts of many historians working on different problems and with different kinds of materials.

· · ·

Similarly, there is nothing preconcerted or designed in a second general tendency that is now rapidly developing. It concerns spatial relationships rather than the relationship between different orders of events.

A striking aspect of recent historical scholarship is the speed with which certain key developments have swept through centers of research and among individual historians throughout the Western world. The study of family history in its modern form is usually thought to have originated with French scholars building on a long tradition of research in demography. The subject was picked up in England, where David Glass and others had been studying population trends in early modern history but without focusing on the sociological questions probed by the French, and was then developed with remarkable enterprise and imagination—promoted with nothing less than missionary zeal—at the University of Cambridge. From there it spread to the United States, where some had already been considering the same questions of structure and magnitudes and what might be called the social psychology of the family. Once the signals from abroad became more reliable and a technique for assembling statistical information became available, research in the history of the family took off in America and has now developed, in typical American fashion, into a decentralized, undisciplined, highly idiosyncratic but creative academic industry.

All of this cumulating, worldwide work in family history reached Germany, whose excellent genealogical records, enhanced by the Nazis' extraordinary *Ortssippenbücher* written to document "pure Aryan" bloodlines, will contribute significantly to a new level of accomplishment in this kind of study.

What happened in family history happened too in historical community studies, in the study of modernization, in the history of social structures, and in the excavation of the buried details of eighteenth-century political thought. Discoveries in one country, in one scholarly culture, quickly affected scholarship advancing in others. Students of American history have good reason, for their own proper work, to examine R. A. Butlin's survey of Irish towns and Gerald L. Soliday's report on Marburg in Upper Hesse; to compare local community controls in Germany, as described in Mack Walker's *German Home Towns,* with those of England; to consider Étienne François's account of the lower classes and poverty in the Rhenish court towns together with Olwen Hufton's *The Poor of Eighteenth-Century France* when assessing Alice Hanson Jones's *Wealth of a Nation to Be: The American Colonies on the Eve of the Revolution;* to examine as a basis for comparison with their own materials the publications on migration patterns in Scandinavia and the many works on Spanish migration; and to ponder Franco Venturi's writings on Beccaria's pamphlet *On*

Crimes and Punishments (1764), so popular and relevant in late-eighteenth-century America, though it originated as a polemic in the altogether different world of Habsburg Milan, dominated by a hereditary patriciate allied to the nobility and the Catholic Church.[3]

There is nothing new in kind in this transnational communication and interaction. Historical scholarship has always been an international enterprise. But seldom has communication been as direct and continuous as it now is. And, more important, never, as far as I know, has the availability of comparable information from far-distant areas in itself reinforced so naturally a major analytical concept. For what is emerging from all of this transnational communication of parallel information is not merely a catalogue of differences and similarities and not simply a progressive sophistication of technique by the application of many minds working in different traditions on similar problems, but something more important: the sense of large-scale systems of events operating over various areas. A rescaling of perspective is taking place in which the basic unit of discussion is larger than any of the traditional units within which research began. Large-scale orbits developing through time have become visible, and within them patterns of filiation and derivation.

Since my interests focus on the Anglo-American world in the early modern period, I naturally became aware of this kind of configuration in that connection. My first inkling of what would develop in this aspect of historical study came over twenty-five years ago in casual conversations with a colleague expert in the Scottish Enlightenment. It became apparent to us as we talked not simply that the leaders of Revolutionary America and of Enlightenment Scotland shared certain ideas but that the distinctively developing cultures in the two countries were fundamentally shaped by similar relationships to a single, central cultural core, in London. This common marginality—a similar distance from and involvement with the same central core—was a shaping element in the growth of each of these provincial cultures and was necessary to explain both. We tried to draw out the implications of this observation, convinced that the formulation was correct, but we did not then realize the magnitude of the issues. We did not know how our literary data related to an overall British Atlantic social system or what other kinds of events and documentation might be seen to be involved in this system. Indeed, we did not know what kind of a system, one small corner of which we were examining, this really was.[4]

At about the same time, David Quinn began publishing some unusually suggestive studies of England's overseas expansion and settlement in the sixteenth century. In them he noted, first, that many of those who were involved in settlements in Ireland were also involved in settlements in America; and, second, that the attitude of the English to natives encountered in these two colonial areas was remarkably similar, and that experience gained in one area was automatically applied in the other. From Quinn's writing alone one began to see the origins of England's Atlantic empire, which included the British Isles themselves as well as overseas territories. What was involved was an expansion of the English, later British, world from its core in southeastern England out into a series of expanding alien peripheries—Wales and the North Country of England in the sixteenth century, Scotland, Ireland, North America, and the Caribbean in the seventeenth century. Phrases linking various British overseas territories, scarcely noticed before, suddenly took on heavy meaning: Ireland was described in a travel book of 1617, for example, as "this famous island in the *Virginian* sea."[5] One could envision a huge, outwardly expanding peripheral arc sweeping north and west from London and the Home Counties into Wales and Lowland Scotland, across Ireland, southwest through Newfoundland, then down the North American coast through Nova Scotia, New England, the Chesapeake, and the Carolinas, and ending in the many Anglo-American settlements in the Caribbean.

This arc was nothing so simple as the trade route of an early empire in the traditional sense, commercial or territorial. Nor was it merely an expanding frontier line. It was not a line, an edge, comprehensible in Turnerian terms as such, but a ring of territories, of marchlands—territories linked to a single overall system designated "British."

But even broadened out to all of these magnitudes, one's vision proved to be too restricted. It remained for J. G. A. Pocock, a New Zealander educated in England and long resident in the United States, to suggest that this entire interactive Atlantic culture system, this huge band of variant marchlands, was in itself only a segment of a global system that ultimately reached Southeast Asia, Australia, New Zealand, and other parts of the Pacific world as well.[6]

The ramifications of such a view are extensive and important. Issues arising in various locations within the periphery which once seemed disparate and discrete can now be seen to have been closely related, and the relationships help explain the course of events. In this perspective, for example, it becomes apparent that official British policy, promulgated in London, restraining the settlement of the trans-Appalachian West in America was shaped in part by the fear of Scottish and absentee Irish landlords in high office in London that their lands would be depopulated by the extension of settlement in America and hence that the economic stability of their lives would be threatened as Americans migrated west into areas four thousand miles from Whitehall. One suddenly understands the reach and penetration of Dr. Johnson's imagination when he observed, on his tour of the western Scottish islands in 1773, that the attraction of the American frontier to discontented Highlanders on the Scottish frontier was a threat to the survival of British culture. Highlanders relocated on the far western British periphery, he said, will simply be lost to the nation: "For a nation scattered in the boundless regions of America resembles rays diverging from a focus. All the rays remain but the heat is gone. Their power consisted in their concentration: when they are dispersed, they have no effect."[7]

Was such a dispersal outward from the center to the margins, with its attendant loss of "concentration," wise? Could it be stopped? Could British law be used to prevent the circulation of British people along the peripheries of British territory? What should be the proper relationships of the outer boundaries to each other and to the core? These problems, which take on meaning only insofar as one grasps not just the eighteenth-century American frontier but the British world system in its entirety, were being discussed actively at the highest level of the British government in November and December 1773, and were at the point of resolution in a controversial proposal that Parliament prohibit further British migration to America, when the conflict between Britain and the colonies put an end to the discussion.

Migration and the problem of the imperial constitution are two aspects of the general issue of core-periphery relations in the early modern British world; there are others. Political institutions and political ideas whose origins lay in the heartland took on different forms in the differing peripheral settings. The peculiar impact of American circumstances on political forms and ideas emanating from the metropolitan culture of Britain determined the shape of public institutions in the United States. But this pan-Atlantic British system of the early modern period cannot be understood in isolation from certain other large systems of the time. Essential to it are intersections with other systems moving within their own patterns.

An explanation of the population history of British North America in the preindustrial period also involves the depiction of a central European system concentrated in the Upper Rhineland but spreading out northeast to the Danish border, east to Bohemia, and southeast through the Danubian basin to southern Russia. Spin-offs from that distinctive and independently evolving system, whose major flows were eastward into Prussia, the Habsburg lands, and Russia, entered directly into the British galaxy of the eighteenth century as the first of some seventy-five thousand "Germans" (in fact, Swiss and French Protestants from the region of Montbéliard as well as subjects of the German princes) began moving down the Rhine, transshipping at Rotterdam and Cowes to reach the *Insel,* as it was sometimes called in the Rhineland, of *Bintzel-vannier* (Pennsyl-vania).

Not only can one plot the intersection of the central European population system with the British, but one can identify individuals whose role it was to forge links between the two independently moving orbits. Benjamin Furly, William Penn's friend and agent, long resident in Rotterdam—merchant, intellectual, land developer, and defender of liberal causes—was the first of these key figures. But the intersections were not limited to Europe; they involved West Africa as well. For the West African population system too spilled over into segments of the British Atlantic world, which was spreading deep into the Ohio and Mississippi valleys, along the Florida coasts, and within the Maritime Provinces of Canada. To see the whole of the entire set of interrelated systems that impinged on preindustrial America one would have to circle the globe like a satellite and note the simultaneous movement of peoples and cultures across a vast area—an area stretching from the Elbe to the Mississippi and from the North Sea to the Congo.[8]

Such a synoptic view develops most readily from the study of population movements. But the concept of inclusive systems with centers and margins, whose integrity as systems is essential to understanding the individual parts within them, is applicable in many spheres.

It has proved effective in intellectual history, most notably in two series of distinguished publications. The first is Franco Venturi's description of the radiations of the Enlightenment from its center in Paris to the near peripheries in western Europe—Spain, Italy, Corsica, Austria, Germany, and England—and then to the outer margins in eastern Europe, Russia, and North America. With his exceptional linguistic ability and his broad vision, Venturi was able to show not merely the general penetration of reform ideas into the remote provinces of the Western world but also the specific adaptations of these ideas that were made in different cultures. His elaborate tracing of the circulation of Beccaria's *On Crimes and Punishments* from its origins in Milan through the whole of Europe shows the possibility of this kind of study. The second is Pocock's elaborate tracing of a single body of political thought—the peculiar language and grammar of "civic humanism"—from Florence to England, Scotland, and America. "A 'language' is uncovered in sixteenth-century Florence," Pocock wrote, "and shown becoming first Puritan, then Whig, then American" as it circulated "away from Europe, towards what is least European in the Anglophone (or 'Atlantic') world."[9]

In a different vein, closer to the approach of

François Furet and his collaborators in the collective inquiry *Livre et société,* is Robert Darnton's book on the publishing history and distribution of the *Encyclopédie.* Through an exhaustive examination of the marketing of the quarto edition of the *Encyclopédie,* Darnton traced the distribution of this key work of the Enlightenment—and hence to a significant degree the diffusion of the Enlightenment itself—from the center in Paris to the French provinces and then out to the Low Countries, the Rhineland, "the north European plains to the Scandinavian fiords and the Russian steppes until finally it reached remote outposts like Lex's bookshop in Warsaw and Rudiger's in Moscow." Through Darnton's eyes we can picture volumes being "hauled across the snow from Leipzig [to St. Petersburg] by sled," and moving up the Elbe and the Moldau, across the Alps to Turin, down the Rhône to Marseilles and Genoa, and along the Danube to Pest, "where," Darnton wrote, "Paris seemed centuries away in contrast to the immediacy of the Ottoman Empire and the unremitting warfare on the eastern front of western culture."[10]

A similarly comprehensive view enabled Robert Palmer and, to a lesser extent, Jacques Godechot to grasp as a singular concatenation of events the pan-European and American explosions of "democratic revolutions" of the late eighteenth century. The possibilities have been shown to be rich in other spheres as well—in analyzing the history of domestic politics (notably American Populism) and a wide range of contemporary phenomena: international relations, political geography, the value systems of organized society, urban environments, and the dissemination of art forms, both fine and applied. And other orbits can be envisioned in other connections: news dissemination, technical expertise, literary forms, business practices.[11]

Thus, it seems to me, in the welter of current historical publications, there are not only signs of a deepening interpenetration of latent and manifest events but also the outlines of systems of filiation and derivation among phenomena that once were discussed in isolation from each other. And, third, there is also in motion in current historical writing an intensifying effort to relate the world of interior, subjective experiences to the course of external events.

Long before it became fashionable to talk about the study of *mentalité,* and well before William Langer had challenged historians to take as their next assignment the application of psychoanalytic principles to historical problems,[12] historians had attempted to describe the state of people's awareness. They had sought to depict, however crudely, not only people's ideas and beliefs as expressed in formal discourse but their deeper, interior life: the assumptions, attitudes, fears, expectations, and aspirations that together formed people's private construction of the world, their personal map of reality, their private ordering of life, the meaning they imposed on the stream of experience. But it has always been extremely difficult to probe the strange interior worlds of the past, partly because the historian has no means of inquiring directly into the condition of people's awareness, partly because in the end historians are more interested in communities of people than in unique individuals. The characterization of a community's interior life, even when its members stand alive before one, available for interviewing, polling, and participant observation, is problematic for the anthropologists, sociologists, and psychologists who design methods precisely for such studies. For historians, lacking living subjects and dependent on random documentation, all of the difficulties are compounded.

Occasionally there has been a historian like Johan Huizinga capable of painting a more or less convincing picture of a great transition in a society's perception of the world by an impressionistic study of art forms and by imaginative projection into the likely experiences of everyday life. And there have been books like Oscar Handlin's *The Uprooted* that trace, through empathy and intuition as well as through documentation, the inner lives of generations of people adjusting to new environments. But most such efforts turn into a vague literary impressionism that reveals as much about the author as about the past, or into a study of formal texts that are supposed somehow to add up to a picture of the "mind of the Middle Ages," *l'esprit laïque,* or *l'esprit bourgeois.* Even in what would seem to be the most manageable aspect of the problem—in the biographies of key historical figures whose individual actions unquestionably shaped events and about whom a great deal is known—the difficulties of exploring subjective experience are great. In any case, collective biography is most often the main question for historians, and to probe beyond what people did, wrote, and said to what they experienced, how they felt, and how they comprehended the world remains a major challenge to historical investigation.

In certain areas in recent years historians have made progress in reaching into subjective experience. While technical psychohistory is still more a matter of theoretical discussion by social scientists than of practice by historians, ways have been found to explore public opinion in the past, attitudes of various kinds, and the pervasiveness and circulation of certain key notions. The range of such studies has been broad. Political thought has provided an important entrée. Working out from the strict genealogy of ideas to the broader aspects of political thought where ideas connect with more general social assumptions and attitudes, historians have been able to enter private worlds otherwise closed to them. So Gordon Schochet's *Patriarchal-*

ism is ostensibly a study in "political thought," but in fact it relates a key concept in political thought to deep-lying social attitudes shared as interior experiences by whole populations in the seventeenth century. W. H. Greenleaf's *Order, Empiricism, and Politics* is also explicitly a study in political thought, but in fact it explores certain presumptions concerning the nature of reality in the broadest sense, the "great hinterland" of beliefs, attitudes, ideas, and assumptions experienced by whole populations. So too, in different ways, do the books and articles of a whole squadron of writers on political "ideology" involved in the American, French, and Russian revolutions.[13]

And other, even more original and imaginative ways have been found to enter the realm of interior experience. Some of the most interesting have reached into nonverbal expressions of private experience and established subtle connections between nonverbal and verbal communication. Carl Schorske's *Fin-de-Siècle Vienna,* in which aspects of interior worlds are uncovered through examination of the connections among a variety of expressions of art forms, has set an attractive new style in scholarship. Schorske's deliberate fusings of urban architecture and political attitudes, of painting and "the liberal ego," and of the descriptive and metaphoric meanings of the garden—these connections among art forms and public life, constructed into a general picture of a community's "psyche," are being emulated and seem destined to shape the work of many historians of culture seeking a deeper understanding of human experience than traditional historical analysis provides. Schorske's style was in fact influential even before his book appeared. Six years earlier his student William McGrath published *Dionysian Art and Populist Politics in Austria,* which not only demonstrates the common pan-Germanist roots of both Viktor Adler's socialism and Gustav Mahler's music and "meta-musical cosmos" (passages from the score of Mahler's Third Symphony precede a chapter on the Liberals' Linz Program) but locates the exact origins of all of these diverging lines of history in the shared outlook, the common interior world, of a particular circle of students in the 1870s, a circle that first formed in a single secondary school, Vienna's Schottengymnasium, and then in a political club at the University of Vienna.[14] These writings on the German-speaking world of the late nineteenth and early twentieth centuries, writings that are beginning to form a genre of their own, may one day be brought into useful comparisons with accounts of similar circles in other cultures: Bloomsbury, Yeats's Dublin, or Herzen's world of Russian exiles in London, for example, circles with distinctive sensibilities, attitudes, and world views. And, indeed, it may be possible to depict the cultural history of an entire era in terms of key "circles" of shared feelings and outlooks.

Studies like Schorske's *Vienna* and McGrath's *Dionysian Art* have concentrated on art forms in probing perceptions of the world, orderings of reality. But the perceptions and orderings that they depict are those of highly cultivated individuals whose relation to ordinary experience may be remote. Efforts have also been made to compose pictures of the inner experiences of less cultivated people—to map the private worlds of ordinary people. Recent studies in popular culture based on nonverbal, behavioral expressions have been revealing—studies like those of Natalie Zemon Davis on the festivals of misrule in sixteenth-century France, of Rhys Isaac on the political theater of eighteenth-century Virginia, and of John Brewer on popular mock elections in Georgian England, a work whose main sources are satirical prints.[15]

But the most extreme and impressive examples are found in two areas. The first is in nineteenth-century French history: in Theodore Zeldin's extraordinary account of "the common beliefs, attitudes and values of Frenchmen," their "unspoken assumptions," their "ambitions, human relationships and the forces which influenced thinking"; and in Guy Thuillier's exploration of the color, sound, taste, pace, and tactile feel of the life of ordinary people in Nevers—the *invisible quotidien* of existence, seen in the use of water, personal hygiene, the pattern of rising and retiring, the "archaeology of gestures," all of which he drew from documents buried accidentally, like tiny chips of stone, in the vast landscape of the past. The second area lies in the exploration of religious sensibilities in the widest and subtlest sense, ranging from Norman Cohn's *Pursuit of the Millennium,* on medieval chiliastic movements, and Perry Miller's volumes on the anatomy of the New England mind, to the remarkable studies by Keith Thomas and Alan Macfarlane on the psychology and sociology of witchcraft and magic in early modern England. These are pathbreaking books, rich and carefully nuanced.[16]

At the level, then, simply of the depiction of interior worlds—patterns of attitudes, beliefs, fears, and aspirations that together organize people's engagement with the exterior world—progress has been made, and there is no question, it seems to me, that we will see much more of this kind of history, ranging from further studies in political ideology to an expanded cartography of the *invisible quotidien* and of religious sensibilities. But in the end the question historians must answer is the relation of these interior worlds to the exterior world of palpable historical events. How is this area of private history, reflecting interior states of awareness, to be related to the external course of events in the past, events of a public nature? To leave these private worlds isolated from the public—to keep the internal separated from the external and to ignore the problem of the effects of the one upon the other—is to evade the central obligation of history, which is to describe how and explain why the course of events took the path it did.

There is no issue of principle here. Obviously what people did was related to what they carried about in their heads: their feelings, their attitudes, their construction of reality. This is obvious in studying individuals, but in studying "peoples" the question skitters off into "climates of opinion" vaguely, if at all, related to the determination of specific events. The problem is inescapable, however, and more and more, in the years ahead, historians will seek answers. They will, that is, seek connections between interior world views—shared attitudes and "mind-sets"—and the course of external events. But, as responses to recent forays into this terrain at the rather obvious level of exploring the "ideological origins" of certain major political events have indicated, establishing the relation of outward events to the submerged world of private awareness is difficult and bound to be controversial.

Thus, within the great mass of contemporary historiography there are, it seems to me, at least three general trends in motion, three lines of development which will in varying ways enrich, but also complicate, any comprehensive accounts that are written: the fusion of latent and manifest events; the depiction of large-scale spheres and systems; and the description of internal states of mind and their relation to external circumstances and events. None of this, of course, is wholly new. Each has anticipations and early formulations, like Karl Lamprecht's advocacy, a century ago, of a historiography explicitly and "scientifically" concentrated on collective psychology and internal states of awareness, a search for the "*Seelenleben,* the psychic life, psychic activity, psychic state" of the German *Volk,* which led him into studies of individual as well as collective consciousness of all kinds.[17] But these anticipations of the present ferment in history were either isolated, programmatic, or metahistorical, or they were caught up in heady delusions about history becoming a "science"—a notion that has persisted, in varying forms, from Lamprecht's time and before through the New Historians of the early twentieth century, to receive what one hopes will be its terminal apotheosis as cliometrics at the hands of Robert Fogel.[18]

What distinguishes the present developments I have sketched is that they are substantive, not merely exhortative. Further, the works involved are not isolated probes by uniquely imaginative individuals but the cumulating work of many historians. The greatest challenge that will face historians in the years ahead, it seems to me, is not how to deepen and further sophisticate their technical probes of life in the past (that effort will, and of course should, continue in any case) but how to put the story together again, now with a complexity and an analytic dimension not envisioned before; how to draw together the information available (quantitative and qualitative, statistical and literary, visual and oral) into readable accounts of major developments. These histories will incorporate anecdote, but they will not be essentially anecdotal; they will include static, "motionless" portrayals of situations, circumstances, and points of view of the past, but they will be essentially dynamic; they will concentrate on change, transition, and the passage of time; and they will show how major aspects of the present world were shaped—acquired their character—in the process of their emergence. No effective historian of the future can be innocent of statistics, and indeed he or she should probably be a literate amateur economist, psychologist, anthropologist, sociologist, and geographer. In the end, however, historians must be not analysts of isolated technical problems abstracted from the past but narrators of worlds in motion—worlds as complex, unpredictable, and transient as our own.

4

History and the Creative Imagination

Historical study is undergoing an enormous expansion in all directions—literary, political, scientific, economic, and social. Whole new modes of study have suddenly appeared on the horizon—QUASSH (quantitative social scientific history), which is so well established that you can get a Ph.D. in it; *histoire totale,* a standard enthusiasm among French historians; ethnographic history; deconstruction studies in legal history. A creative time in history, but yet a confusing time, which calls for an occasional reassessment not of the new trends but of the permanent underpinnings, the essentials that simply inhere in the craft by virtue of its nature.

Hence my purpose: to attempt to isolate, amid all this tumult, the creative process in historical study. What is creativity in history? I do not mean, what is the most widely read kind of history, important as that is. I ask simply what has transformed the subject and shifted it to a new plane of understanding. What kind of historians are creative in that sense? What is it essentially that they do? How do they do it? How do their publications differ from other good and useful history that adds to knowledge and commands interest and respect but that does not transform the subject?

In order to do this I would like to turn to the work of a very few modern historians, mostly of the past generation, whose scholarship has been, beyond dispute, creative. I want to look at extreme cases—of historians whose writing shifted the direction of historical inquiry not by exhortation but by substantive and enduring discovery—and find, if I can, in these dilated cases, ingredients that are necessary in some measure for all creative efforts in history, and perhaps in other fields as well. For others of us of lesser creative force will show the same characteristics in lesser degree. Reputation does not interest me, though the historians I have chosen achieved a full measure of recognition in their lifetimes; nor does sheer extent of productivity. What I am looking for is the capacity to enrich a whole area of history by redirecting it from established channels into new directions, unexplored directions, so that what was once vague or altogether unperceived is suddenly flooded with light, and the possibilities of a new way of understanding are suddenly revealed. I am looking for redirectors of inquiry, those whose work made a difference without which our present understanding would be impossible.

My selection may seem arbitrary or at least too

personal. But it is precisely cases personally close to me that I want. My purpose requires intimacy, because I want to get below the surface, to isolate, if I can, some of the essential inner qualities of creativity, and to isolate as well the problems and limitations which inevitably accompany such creative efforts, and for that I need to know my subjects well. And I need to have a good spread in types of history—political, sociopolitical, institutional, administrative, intellectual.

My first choice is certainly a very personal one. My late teacher and colleague Perry Miller not only transformed the study of Puritanism in seventeenth-century New England but shifted the balance of American intellectual history in permanent ways. It is not simply that he found the Puritan thinkers profound and original and made them attractive to others. Beyond that, he laid the foundations of his own structure of American intellectual history, and in the process elevated the subject to a new, more sophisticated plane where historians, as Edmund Morgan wrote, became philosophers and philosophers were obliged to become historians.

The achievement of my second exemplar lay not in intellectual history but, though it ranged widely, primarily in administrative and institutional history. Charles McLean Andrews, whose major publications number 102 items, 23 of them books, and whose minor publications number no fewer than 360 items, concentrated his most mature work and had his most creative impact in the area of Anglo-American institutional and administrative relations in the seventeenth and eighteenth centuries. His masterpiece is the four-volume *Colonial Period of American History* (1934–38), which recounts in great detail the development of public institutions in the settlement and growth of the American colonies and, in volume 4, the administrative structure of the Anglo-American empire in the eighteenth century. When his work was done, the subject had been transformed. One could never thereafter think of the origins of American public institutions as some kind of transfer of seeds from Germanic origins, as Andrews's teachers had thought of it, or as a natural American product, as the Turnerites would have it, but as a quite traceable evolution of transplanted British institutions.

My third choice is more famous the world around than Andrews, and he was far more important a public polemicist and public actor than either Miller or Andrews. Nevertheless, he was a creative scholar in the same measure as they, and a more expressive literary craftsman, despite his non-English-speaking origins. Lewis Namier, born in Russian Poland, had a curious and complex career. At one time or another he was a civil servant in the British propaganda

department and in the political intelligence department of the Foreign Office, a businessman, an independent scholar, a top executive of the world Zionist
movement, and finally, starting in 1931, a professor
of history at the University of Manchester. His two
main books, *The Structure of Politics at the Accession of
George III* and *England in the Age of the American Revolution,* were published in 1929 and 1930. By the time
he died in 1960 (three years before Miller's death and
seventeen years after Andrews's), he was generally
recognized as one of the most powerful minds in the
Anglophone historical world, a "titanic" figure, in
J. H. Plumb's phrase, and as the architect of one of its
most imposing edifices. His great achievement was to
recast the structure of British political history. Concentrating his interests on the early years of the reign
of George III, he destroyed the notions of the whiggish historians of the nineteenth century, whose views
had prevailed until then, that British political history
is a tale of the gradual growth and triumph of liberal parliamentary democracy, a victory that moved
forward through dialectical struggles of the Whig
and Tory parties, inspired by different basic beliefs.
Namier put the political system of the 1760s under
microscopic examination, and concluded that what
mattered were not the struggles between Whig and
Tory party organizations or their partisans' beliefs but
complex networks of "connections," interests, client-

age, and personal dependency, all drawn together into a fluctuating government by the power of patronage. Once he had published his major works, the genealogy of British party history had to be recast, its character rethought.

My final exemplar is anomalous, in that his work lies in a field far from the area of my own research, and while I have studied his main work with care, I have to rely in part, in speaking of him, on the authority of experts in that field. But Ronald Syme is surely one of the most creative forces in twentieth-century historiography, and his monumental work in ancient history and in classical studies generally, particularly his *Roman Revolution,* has exerted the same creative effect as Miller's *New England Mind,* Andrews's *Colonial Period,* and Namier's *Structure of Politics.* He was a young man—thirty-six—when his *Roman Revolution* was published in 1939, but its recognition was delayed by the war. Its impact was felt profoundly, however, in the years that followed. Classicists first, and then historians generally, recognized its transforming impact on the entire formulation of the transition from republic to empire in Roman history. *The Roman Revolution* came as a "realist" shock. The venerable constitutional legalisms simply faded away. The reality of Roman political history became not a struggle between Senate and People, between *Optimates* and *Populares,* or between *nobiles* and *novi homines.* The reality was the buildup of Augustus's autocratic power achieved duplicitously, in the words of Syme's distinguished former student Glen Bowersock, "through a nexus of marriages and client relationships among the old and new aristocrats of Rome."

For Syme, through a miracle of prosopographical research, traced the family connections of every individual who played a role in Roman politics during the late Republic and the early Principate—say, 60 B.C. to A.D. 14. He discovered that "the composition of the oligarchy of government" changed, was constantly being reconstituted largely by the revivifying of Rome's decaying aristocratic families and recruitment of new families from the provinces. The familiar story of Roman politics and constitutionalism became unfamiliar, became new and surprising, as Syme reinterpreted the course of events as a function of clientage and family ties. The technical heart of the book lies in Syme's mastery of the collective biographies of the entire politically active population of Rome. This triumph of Roman prosopography is vividly displayed in *The Roman Revolution*'s seven foldout genealogical tables that trace the politically significant family ties and offices of the Metelli, the kinsmen of Cato, the family of Augustus, the Aemilii Lepidi, the descendants of Pompeius, the family of Sejanus, and the connections of Varus.

Here then is my cast of characters—Miller, Andrews, Namier, and Syme—and it is in their work and careers that I hope to find some clues to the nature and characteristics of creativity in historical scholarship. Other historians, of classic fame, might have been chosen. But the circumstances of research and writing were truly different in far different times and places. The historians I am talking about are people of our own time and culture who have transformed the subject they studied under conditions of life and technical demands familiar to us all. But even of contemporaries, others might well have been chosen. Still, let us make do with the four I have chosen, and try to isolate in them some, at least, of the critical elements of creativity, and by that means seek to identify essential characteristics of historical study in general, for all of us in some degree, for them in supreme measure, under present-day conditions.

The first task, it seems to me, is the most difficult. It is to identify the general quality of mind and imagination that went into the writing of the four masterworks: *The New England Mind, The Colonial Period in American History, The Structure of Politics,* and *The Roman Revolution.* All are big learned works. But what sustains the labor behind such works as these is no mere love of detail and no simple instinct for beaver-like industry. These learned historians did not simply lay out information and they did not write straightforward traditional narratives, though the narratives that would follow would be written on the basis of these new foundations. Namier never wrote a sustained narrative; his history is almost entirely analytic. Syme did write a narrative of politics but, as he recognized himself, as a political story it is at times difficult to follow because of the multitude of detailed references. It is further complicated by Syme's prose style, modeled in part on Tacitus's Latin style. It is tightly compacted, abrupt, dense, and allusive. Andrews, it must be said, was a dutiful but dull narrator. And as for Perry Miller's narrative prose, it might best be described as compelling and elusive. His thought—the exposition—swirls around and around like a figure skater, tracing all sorts of delicate and intricate movements, ending in a graceful conclusion. It's all a vivid spectacle and wonderful to watch, but in the end it is sometimes difficult to figure out what exactly has happened.

Thus in a critical passage in the second volume of *The New England Mind,* Miller writes, "We may look upon October 19, 1652, as crucial in American history." Now one startles at that, and reads quickly on to see what heads rolled on that remarkable day, what fateful decisions were made or grim conclusions reached. It turns out to be the day on which the Massachusetts General Court ordained a fast—which was unremarkable in itself, except that the reasons given for proclaiming the fast involved "a profound shift of emphasis." So the event is a shift of emphasis. Unfortunately, this shift of emphasis, Miller then explains, was "so imperceptible that it might have been merely careless phraseology—except that the tendency, once started, gathered momentum." Momentum, yes, but slow momentum, it turns out, and subtle indeed. "Within another ten years," Miller could see (though not apparently all the Puritans, and not all of Miller's attentive readers) that "the formula was completely transformed."

Now, I suggest that the onset of a shift of emphasis and the slow and subtle transformation of a formula is no doubt an event, of sorts—and this is narrative writing, of sorts. But it surely does not explain Miller's power as a historian.

What distinguishes their work—the essence of it, I believe—is, in the end, the capacity to conceive of a hitherto unglimpsed world, or of a world only vaguely and imperfectly seen before. Each of these historians at some point acquired a vision of a world that in the received literature had been submerged beneath abstractions and generalities or otherwise obscured. It is as if they had been circling a world blocked from view by clouds through which only occasionally could be glimpsed patches of blue sea, green and brown earth, and from these occasional glimpses of reality they had sensed, had pictured, and then had conceived whole, the entire world that lay below.

So Miller, having plunged into the mass of Puritan writings previously ignored as second-rate theology, projected an edifice of the intellect whose foundations lay deep in the soil of the Protestant Reformation. Andrews saw beneath vague generalities of Anglo-American governance an intricate network, a living, functioning world, of committees and Boards of Trade, of administrative procedures, of laws and charters and memos, and bundles of reports and notes and papers being passed from office to office, from official to official—all of which composed for him a coherent picture of a responsible empire of the English-speaking peoples. So Namier saw beneath the traditional story of Whigs and Tories, liberalism and autocracy, competing ideologies, and party rivalries a world of shifting patronage clusters, which together formed the loose and fluctuating coalitions that governed Britain. And so Syme (who had not read anything by Namier before he wrote *The Roman Revolution*) saw beneath the façade of a supposed legitimate constitutional settlement after the civil wars a multitude of binding personal ties among the oligarchy in Rome and their recruits from the provinces who together formed a tightly held autocratic power center dominated by Augustus that ruled an empire encompassing most of the Western world.

What is the quality of mind and imagination that went into these imaginative projections? How did they make these designs of past worlds? Here the classical cases may help: Gibbon, sitting "amidst the ruins of the Capitol" "while the barefooted friars were singing vespers in [what had been] the temple of Jupiter," and projecting from that bizarre anomaly his whole vast conception of the decline and fall of the Roman empire. Or Macaulay, steeped in the novels of Walter Scott, daydreaming, "castle-building," as we know from John Clive's biography, with his beloved sisters, projecting imaginary worlds, imaginary speeches, and portentous events, which later in his volumes became clothed with the reality of the reign of James II and William III in the pages of his *History of England*.

There is something romantic in the imaginings of these two earlier historians; and I suggest that the same is true of our hardheaded, technically masterful, myth-destroying modern quadrumvirate. No one who ever saw Perry Miller striding across the Harvard Yard, belted up in an Army trench coat, will ever doubt that there lay within a romantic soul, imagining, self-dramatizing. And if one missed this picture, one could find it in another form in Miller's own account of the origins of his life work, in which he identifies himself with Gibbon in the moment of conception of *The Decline and Fall,* but with an ironic twist. "It was given to me," Miller wrote in 1956, "on the edge of a jungle of central Africa, to have thrust upon me the mission of expanding what I took to be the innermost propulsion of the United States, while supervising, in that barbaric tropic, the unloading of drums of case oil flowing out of the inexhaustible wilderness of America." It was, he said, that "vision" and that theme that possessed him. "What I believe caught my imagination, among the fuel drums, was a realization of the uniqueness of the American experience; even then I could dimly make out the portent for the future of the world, looking upon these tangible symbols of the Republic's appalling power. I could see no way of coping with the problem except by going to the beginning."

Namier too was a romantic, an insecure romantic conservative. "Jew and not Jew," as J. H. Plumb has written, "Pole and not Pole, landowner and not landowner," Namier developed a vision of ultimate stability in Britain's ancient social order and deeply rooted institutions, visible to him in his own time as well as in the late eighteenth century. Andrews? The dispassionate scholar, the self-disciplined Connecticut Yankee, the decorous, apparently unromantic academician? He was born in 1863, and his emotional and intellectual roots lay deep in the late-nineteenth-century struggles over the Anglo-Saxon identity of the United States in the face of the great eastern and southern European immigrations. Andrews was deeply involved in the struggle to assert the essentially Anglian character of American life, and his historical work was a direct expression of that emotional and imaginative projection. It showed in irrefutable detail the roots of his, and the nation's, ethnic identity. And Ronald Syme? One can only guess what subjective meaning the story of the Roman provincials' absorption into the cosmopolis of Rome may have had to this New Zealander who rose through the ranks at Oxford to succeed his teacher, Hugh Last, in the Camden Chair of Ancient History and to acquire a knighthood which Last himself had never received. Among Syme's early unpublished works is a book entitled *The Provincial at Rome,* much of which went into *The Roman Revolution,* and in 1958 he sketched the same theme in broader dimensions in *Colonial Élites: Rome, Spain, and the Americas.*

All of these historians were in some degree emotionally involved in the world they discovered, and all had what George Kitson Clark found most striking in Macaulay: "an imaginative grasp of the historical situation as a whole."

It is the wholeness of their visions, the capacity to conceive of an entire world and not merely one problem or one issue or one theme, that is the crucial element. In this imaginative capacity these historians are comparable, I believe, less to other scholarly historians than to the novelists who have created entire worlds, populated them, furnished them, traced their traumas and triumphs, their growth and decline. Faulkner, for example, conceiving a "mythical kingdom" in a county in northern Mississippi complete with an identifiable population of shopkeepers and mechanics, farmers and tenants and gentry—a county, Malcolm Cowley wrote, with "a population of 15,600 persons scattered over 2400 square miles. It sometimes seems to me that every house or hovel has been described in one of Faulkner's novels; and that all the people of the imaginary county, black and white, townsmen, farmers, and housewives, have played their parts in one connected story." So too the mythical but deeply real world, furnished, populated, and described with exquisite care by Proust; or the nightmare worlds of Dostoevsky, or the social universe of *War and Peace*.

The central instinct, the crucial, necessary "genius," if I may use that word, that lay behind the creative historiography of these immensely energetic and highly technical historians seems to me to have been a kind of literary imagination: the capacity to project, like a novelist, a nonexistent, an impalpable world in all its living comprehension, and yet to do this within the constraints of verifiable facts. I am well aware of the differences between fact and fiction, but I am as much struck by the general historical accuracy of Faulkner's *Absalom, Absalom!* as I am by the visionary structure Perry Miller erected for his history.

This seems to me to be the central, the fundamental element in the accomplishments of these exceptionally creative historians: their capacity to conceive not simply of a new issue here or a fresh problem there, but of a verifiable world of interconnections, of relationships which together add up to a different and better picture of the whole—more comprehensive, deeper, closer to the grain of reality—than had been seen before.

But if, as I believe, this is the fundamental quality of mind that is found in their historical writing, there are other, more specific characteristics as well, closer to the substance of their work.

All four of our historians are contextualists. That is, they sought to understand the past in its own terms: to relocate events, the meaning of documents, the motivations of historical actors in their original historical settings. Their greatest suspicions and vigilance were directed at anachronism. They are forever doubting that words meant then what they mean now, that motivations are always the same, that circumstances repeat themselves significantly. What seem to them most revealing are the differences between past and present, not the similarities; it is the differences that excite their imagination, that suggest the lines of discovery to them. And they were therefore keyed to surprises: it is the capacity for surprise rather than for the satisfaction of familiar recognition that made their work possible.

But their contextualism becomes operative not in the abstract but through data—rich, complex, and above all newly discovered or rediscovered data, to which all of them have an extraordinary sensitivity. They all had the capacity to locate, control, and absorb very large quantities of hitherto unused or underused data. In every case it was the immersion in a mass of new or freshly examined data that allowed them to think creatively. All of them seemed by some remarkable accident (but of course it is no accident) to fall into a mass of fresh archival material.

In Miller's case, it was the library of Puritan writings, almost all of it published but scarcely examined seriously by general historians before. Miller immersed himself in the sermons of the seventeenth-century New England clergy and in the ancillary court records, diaries, and personal correspondences, until he was so completely attuned to the Puritans' way of thinking that he could anticipate whole arguments from a few key words. The rich unexploited archive of Puritan writings was critical. And indeed editing and republishing these documents, or some of them, seemed as necessary to him as it was natural as he developed his views on the Puritans' past. If he had done nothing but publish the anthology of Puritan writings in 1938, with its splendid introductions, he would have transformed the study of Puritanism and indeed of seventeenth-century history in general.

Similarly, Andrews's most creative work grew out of his discovery of the great mass of documentation on eighteenth-century Anglo-American connections contained in the Public Record Office in London, especially the Colonial Office papers, category 5, which he explored year after year. The world he ultimately revealed is the world he discovered in that great treasure house. Again, as in Miller's case, if he had done no more than explore and publicize these documents—which he did in the still fundamental guides to the American materials in the Public Record Office, in the British Museum, in the minor London archives, and in the Oxford and Cambridge libraries—he would have transformed the subject of Anglo-American relations, though at a much slower pace.

So too Namier's *Structure of Politics* emerged from a vast mass of new data—whole archives of letters and memos of the managers of patronage, the "men of business" who served the great public figures, and the party whips and local shire and borough managers from whose intricate maneuverings a mosaic could be constructed of the pattern of political influence. The key documents are the Newcastle Papers—371 volumes of correspondence and notes in the so-called Additional MSS then in the British Museum which Namier studied for the period of his interest microscopically. His sensitive response to this documentation comes out clearly in every page of his major books. He cannot cease quoting, and quoting at length, even in his biographical studies of George III and Charles Townsend.

And as for Syme—his control of the prosopographical sources is simply staggering. He seems to have memorized the entire corpus of German scholarship on family ties among the Roman elite. Without the prosopographical work of Friedrich Münzer, he wrote in the preface of *The Roman Revolution,* "this book could hardly have existed." And beyond that, he went through the whole of classical literature plus official records such as the consular *fasti,* the inscriptions and archaeological data, with a mind capable of total recall and powerfully magnetized to any scrap of data that would show some tie among individuals, some clue to *clientelae,* and that would explain behavior.

Thus, oriented to contexts of the past and immersed in great arrays of data never used in so concentrated a form by historians before, these historians begin their reconstructions. Reacting innocently, as it were, to the new documentation; alert to surprises; their minds skinned open and sensitive to the minu-

tiae of the data, to any peculiarity, anomaly, oddity
that might appear—to anything that does not explain
itself—they start to recompose the world.

Certain repetitions of words strike them as significant. For Miller: "covenant," "preparation." For
Syme, *clientela, factio*—words whose repetition suddenly makes them crucial to the discussion. Once
passed over lightly as commonplace in the documents,
they now seem to leap out from the pages, their recur-
rence the evidence of a meaning previously unknown.

But it is not only certain words that take on heavy
significance. Certain hitherto obscure people are
brought into sudden prominence, as they are seen to
be significant within a different pattern. For Namier,
there were the political brokers: Newcastle above all,
but also the lesser "men of business" for the great
political magnates—Thomas Whately for Grenville,
Barlow Trecothick as well as Edmund Burke for Rock-
ingham, Charles Jenkinson for Bute. For Andrews,
there was a series of busy bureaucrats—amazingly
busy and productive: William Blathwayt, the critically influential member of the Board of Trade for
many years; the Popples, William, William Jr., and
Alured, father, son, and grandson, who successively
held the secretaryship of the Board of Trade. With
their successors, Thomas Hill and John Pownall, the
Popples controlled the paperwork and indirectly
the policies of the British colonial office for almost

a century (1696–1776). They were busy people and extremely influential through their memoranda, their legislative management, and their handling of the vast mass of Anglo-American official correspondence, and they became people of great importance for Andrews. For Miller, Peter Ramus, whose logical system became an antagonist in the story; the theologian William Ames; and a galaxy of previously obscure New England preachers, now seen to be contributors to a great world of the intellect: John Cotton, Richard Mather, Urian Oakes, Samuel Willard, Michael Wigglesworth. For Syme a complex array of key families: sons and cousins, nephews and collateral connections of the great.

These newly exhumed worlds are rich and complex, so rich, so complex that their full exploration proves to be beyond the powers of these generative historians, great as those powers are. They all do attempt in some way to sketch the whole story as they see it—Namier projected his story back hundreds of years in the vast *History of Parliament* project he revived (to date forty-one volumes), identifying the political significance of every individual who ever sat in a session of Parliament. But they must leave much of the work to their followers, and so the challenge of exploring their worlds remains exciting through at least two generations.

In Miller's case, the headquarters of further exploration shifted from Harvard to Yale where, under Edmund Morgan, a small but powerful industry developed, with essays and books flowing out year after year on the intellectual world that Miller discovered, until the work approached a kind of intellection more rigorous in its demands, more learned, than anything the Puritans themselves could easily have coped with. So too Andrews's followers and developers went beyond him in fields that he discovered, and the "Namier school" became notorious. "The most powerfully organized squadron in our historical world at the present time," Herbert Butterfield wrote. It was in fact small in number—six or seven young historians—but all of them were energetic and prolific. Syme too had few doctoral students, but they formed a powerful international group—Germans, Scots, Americans, Canadians—whose influence radiated out broadly to the greater world.

To these followers the excitement of recording and developing the newly discovered world was contagious. The work fructified, expanded, and for a while carried all before it, until finally, at the end of their careers, these masters ran into boundary problems—spatial, temporal, methodological. At that point a new phase set in.

The original discoverers themselves were seldom the leaders in establishing the boundary conditions.

Gripped by the new ideas, the new ways of interpreting a large area of history, they were intent on reconstructing the entire world as far as they could, and in their creative tumult it was difficult for them even to see the boundaries. The very force and impetus of their discoveries, the excitement of progressive, cumulative, seemingly boundless revelation carried them and their first sympathizers and coworkers beyond their immediate materials into areas and issues they could not fully control. And so, whether they were aware of it or not, in the process of expansion they revealed the effective limits on their own discoveries. Opposition developed as these boundaries became understood—at times quite bitter opposition.

Take the case of Namier. Two important historians have viciously declared the boundaries. The first was Butterfield. It is doubtful if there is an indictment of any historian as bitter as Butterfield's attack on "the Namier school" in his book *George III and the Historians*. Where, Butterfield demanded to know in one hundred pages of blistering criticism, are the *issues* of politics; where are the *beliefs;* where is the *story* of what happened? "Over and above the structure of polities," he wrote, "we must have a political history . . . in which (no matter how much we know about the structure of polities and the conditions of the time) we can never quite guess, at any given moment, what is going to happen next." Everything in Namier's account, Butterfield argued, is atomized; men act only to enjoy profit and places; corruption is made to explain everything in the House of Commons. But surely there is chance, surely there are ideas as well as structure in the determination of history. "If we carry the idea of Sir Lewis Namier to an extreme it is difficult to see why the study of history—a history so woven out of chances and ironies of circumstance—should be considered an important matter for anybody." There is value, he conceded, in the Namierite revolution, but what that value really is will remain hidden until the rest of history, banished by Namier, is put back in.

The second major critic was J. H. Plumb, who set the temporal boundaries. In his Ford Lectures, *The Growth of Political Stability in England 1675–1725,* and in the writings of his students examining the politics of the late seventeenth and eighteenth centuries, Plumb revealed a world far different from Namier's. In the early eighteenth century ideas did count for a great deal, and Whigs and Tories did fight in much the way Macaulay had said they did. In other words, Namier had described (Plumb explained) not a political world that had existed back to the beginning of politics, but a world that had originated in the mid-eighteenth century and ended at a particular time. For the farther boundaries in the 1780s too were being marked, by Ian Christie and others, while the existence of party and ideology in the mid-eighteenth century was being explored by Plumb's students John Brewer and Linda Colley. Namier's world, therefore, proved to be a brief one, lasting from the 1730s until the 1780s, and never in the pure form he imagined. It was always interpenetrated with some measure of the ingredients he had denied.

A parallel can be found in the historiography of Roman history. Arnold Toynbee was one of a half-dozen shrill critics of Syme. "Able and active minds," Toynbee wrote of Syme, "reduced to a starvation-diet of knowledge, have fallen greedily upon the additional fare that the 'prosopographical' approach to Roman history offers; and they have been under a constant temptation to read more into the evidence of this sort than can truly be found in it." Apply Syme's method, Toynbee suggested, to your own circle of living people, where one has more information than "dry and jejune . . . notices of births, marriages, deaths, appointments, and elections," and you will see the limitations.

In Miller's case the boundaries were more subtle, but they were gradually worked out, largely from within the fellowship of faithful followers—to the point where, as one recent writer put it, there developed a "ritual patricidal totem feast." Critical comments (though usually respectful, even admiring) came in from all sides—from former students, coworkers in Puritan studies, and specialists in intellectual history, questioning some of the foundations of Miller's views: the originality he attributed to the Puritans' thought, his belief in the Puritans' influence on the deep trends in America's history and "destiny" and in their success in reconciling piety and intellect, in the end the validity of the entire concept of a collective "mind."

The boundaries in Andrews's case are particularly interesting since they were encountered, with some bewilderment, by Andrews himself. At the end of his life he recognized only too well that his huge new world of Anglo-American administration had ignored the whole realm of social history, which surely was relevant in some way—though how, he did not know—and further, that he had not dealt with politics as such, only with government. One realizes as one reads the poignant memoir he left unpublished at his death that he lacked the conceptual ability to deal with both politics and society and to integrate them into his institutional and administrative world.

Nothing in Andrews's training and nothing he could later devise for himself furnished tools with which to analyze the social context of public life. He pondered inconclusively the character of social history. His original plan for the projected seven volumes of *The Colonial Period* included one on "colonial life in the eighteenth century." But, as he freely admitted and as one of his poorer books, *Colonial Folkways,* clearly attests, he never found in social history what he wisely knew to be a prime necessity for historical analysis, "logical or synthetical form." Social history appeared to him either as "a sort of chaos of habits and customs, ways of living, dressing, eating, and the performance of duties of existence"—a "disorganized mass of half-truths"—or as "social science," dealing not with development in time but with the laws of human behavior. Neither was acceptable to him.

Yet this was an area that was stirring with new life when Andrews's big volumes were being written. Twenty years after his death in 1944, another new world was developing in precisely those areas, glowing into reality beneath the one he himself had first developed. A cluster of younger historians suddenly saw his once exciting institutional and administrative structures as fusty and superficial. The administrative structure that he had explained was certainly there, but what had driven it? What gave it life? The shaping forces, it seemed, had been ignored. Quickly, in the generation that followed Andrews's, the politics of empire, which Andrews had never broached, was sketched by young scholars. And the underlying social history, which Andrews knew to be basic but could not grasp, lay waiting to be brought together within an effective framework of ideas.

All of this, in outline form, seems to me to constitute the creative process in historical scholarship.

Let me put it together. Creativity begins in the imaginative grasp of a world of relationships hitherto obscured by clouds of received notions. Anomalies in the received tradition are detected, discrepancies observed, and then one discovers a complete and integrated world that had lain hidden—complex, multitudinous: like the fictional worlds of Proust and Faulkner. In rising excitement the discoverer sets out to explore it all, to show its details, its interconnections, and its vitality. That recovery of a hitherto submerged world, and the capacity to conceive of it as a whole, form the essence of historical creativity, and it has certain necessary attributes.

(1) It develops out of a contextualist sense— out of a desire to remove the anachronistic overlays imposed on the real past by previous historians: presentist falsifications which these historians believe they are themselves free of.

(2) It develops by the exploitation of newly found or newly investigated data, massive data, which allow extensive exploration of

a large realm of human experience in the past.

(3) It develops through a process of sensitive identification of key phrases, of key figures, key events, which together form as it were a diagram of the essential relationships.

All of this is dynamic, exciting, revealing; and it seems for a time to be boundless. The progenitors explore wide reaches of their new terrain, but despite their energy and enthusiasm they cannot encompass it all. Their followers go further, see more, until they encounter boundary problems—temporal, spatial, intellectual, methodological. Criticism becomes sharp; and finally the true shape of the newly discovered world is firmly depicted. Its irreducible substance proves to be far more than a previous generation had dreamed of, but something less than the discoverers, at the height of their powers, believed they had seen, spread out before them.

5

The Losers

The historical writings on the loyalists—the Americans who stood by Britain during and after the Revolution—are replete with logical dilemmas, rhetorical excesses, and strange silences. For a full century they were less history than reflections of the authors' search for personal identity in a swiftly changing world, or veiled political arguments, or expressions of ethnic anguish. There is no better example of history as "relevant"—of history as an expression of the authors' personal concerns, of history that had to come out right. In the history of historical writing it is a strange and intriguing episode.

The first phase of interpretation of the loyalists was dominated by participants in the Revolution or their immediate successors, hence writers who were still part of the Revolution itself, and fiercely polemical. The patriots' chroniclers—Mercy Otis Warren, David Ramsay, and William Gordon[1]—eager to establish the righteousness of the American cause, seized the historiographical initiative and portrayed the loyalists as betrayers of their homeland, sycophants of ruling aristocrats, unnatural sons, traitors. Any impulse that might have been felt to explain the popularity or the logic of the loyalist opposition to the Revolution was constrained by a logical embarrassment. The central object of these first, patriotic chroniclers of the Revolution was to prove that the Revolution was not just a contested party victory but a spontaneous uprising of the entire population. The dignity of the new nation was involved, and there was no desire to make sense of the Americans who had opposed the creation of the nation, or even to notice their existence. And when, during the first party battles of the post-Revolutionary period, the very survival of the nation seemed to be at stake, what purpose could be served by proving that the birth of the United States had been fiercely opposed by a sizable and highly placed segment of the American population and that the Revolution's aims had not been shared by important American leaders? So the historical heroics of this earliest, myth-making period were grotesquely exaggerated: the Founding Fathers were portrayed as flawless paragons commanding the almost universal allegiance of the population, and those loyalists who could not be totally ignored were blasted as parasites typical of the worst corruptions of the *ancien régime*.

None of this is particularly surprising. What is surprising is that these wildly patriotic histories so completely engrossed the field. There were no counter-heroics to match; no contemporary writing that presented the opposite view in equally polemical terms. The explanation of this important fact leads to the loyalists themselves. For it would surely have been from them that one would have expected such a counter-interpretation of history to come. And indeed one such slashing vilification of the victors was written—by the last royal chief justice of Massachusetts, Peter Oliver. In the war years, 1777 and 1781, he composed, in "the quiet of a small cottage in suburban London," a fierce polemic. But his book lay in manuscript for almost two hundred years, and when it was finally published, in 1961, it proved to be so bizarre in its partisanship that its scholarly editors felt obliged to introduce it with an apologetic explanation of its value as a document of the Revolution.[2] A few other, less vituperative loyalist histories were published in these early years, but none were issued as direct challenges to the patriotic histories; and none attempted to dislodge the patriots' structure of the narrative.[3] The best of the loyalist histories was Thomas Hutchinson's carefully documented chronicle of the Revolutionary movement in Massachusetts, but he deliberately pruned it of all polemics and forbade its publication until both he and his enemies had passed from the scene. Even the loyalists' private journals and letters, which might have served something of the same purpose as chronicles, were withheld from publication until after they could have affected the initial historiographical tradition.[4]

What lay behind this remarkable reticence? The loyalists faced a dilemma in attempting to adjust to their fate. The most distressing element in their lot, the great Whig historian George Otto Trevelyan later wrote in a sympathetic passage, "was that they had always been animated, and now were tortured, by a double patriotism; for they were condemned to stand by, idle and powerless, while the two nations, which they equally loved, were tearing at each other's vitals."

Many were exiled in England, and there they found the English upper classes utterly disdainful of refugee provincials who, the society wit George Selwyn explained, "when people of fashion were mentioned, did not know to what country they belonged, or with what families they were connected; who had never in their lives amused themselves on a Sunday, and not much on any day of the week; who were easily shocked, and whose purses were slender." And they found the common people of England to be even less sympathetic. For they so abused these "damned American rebels" that the loyalists were forced, Trevelyan wrote, "to assume the cudgels against defamers of their nation." Judge Samuel Curwen, once of Salem, Massachusetts, wrote bitterly in his journal in London in 1776 that a returning soldier he met speaks of the Yankees (as he is pleased to call them) in the most contemptuous terms, as cowards and poltroons, or as having as bad quality the depraved heart can be cursed with. . . . It is my earnest wish [that] the despised American may convince these conceited islanders that without regular, standing armies our continent can furnish brave soldiers, judicious, active and expert commanders, [and will do so] by some knockdown, irrefragable argument; . . . not till then may we expect generous treatment. It piques my pride (I confess it) to hear us called, *our colonies and our plantations* as if our property and persons were absolutely theirs, like the villeins and their cottages in the old feudal system.[5]

Curwen and most of the other articulate, informed exiles hoped for nothing so much as a quick end to the war and a settlement that would allow them to return to their homes. Proud of their American identity and fearful of still further antagonizing their countrymen who had banished them, they had no desire to refute the patriot histories publicly. They wrote; but they kept their writing private, and left it to posterity to vindicate the choice they had so fatally made.

Who else was there to bear their banner, to show the reason and humanity that had lain with them in the days when the outcome had still been uncertain, when men of equal virtue and wisdom could differ on the path most proper to take? Their English political allies, the Whig opposition to George III's government? But the loyalists bore living witness against everything the English Whig opposition, presumably sympathetic to the American cause, sought to establish. Stripped of all embellishments, their song had but a single theme: all Americans loved their British homeland; and given a modicum of just and sympathetic governance they would have clung to England forever. Instead, they had in effect been driven out of the empire by the ignorance, folly, venality, and blindness of a gang of ministers who had taken over the reins of government from the weak hands of George III and had driven England back toward that state of autocracy from which it had emerged barely a century before. The loss of the colonies was the result of misdeeds in high places—it was the government's fault, and not something generated in the hearts of Americans themselves or born of the inevitable resentments, the humiliations, of colonial dependence.

Now what good were the loyalists for such a story as this? For years they had claimed the exact opposite. The loyalists had warned again and again, in the years of open controversy, that the true, basic source of the struggle did not lie primarily in the policies of a reactionary ministry. It was not the government's fault—it had been misled. The source of the trouble was the determination of certain discontented and power-hungry Americans to throw off the tie to England as the first step in revolutionizing both government and society. There was nothing accidental in this, the loyalists had explained. The whole upheaval had been planned in the colonies, and no policy of the English government that in any way preserved the empire would have made any difference. But the Whig opposition kept up its cry—half sincere, half opportunistic—that *all* Americans wanted nothing more than an appropriate place in the empire and were being driven out by the ministry. The loyalists were therefore liars or self-seeking hirelings of a ministry whose corrupting influence had seeped into these distant provinces.

It was not the English opposition that set the first important historiographical tradition for interpreting the loyalists, but England's Tory historians of the early nineteenth century: particularly John Adolphus, a lawyer with connections to the conservative government, and Viscount Mahon, later fifth Earl Stanhope, whose seven-volume *History of England . . . 1713–1783* became the standard narrative.

For them sympathy with the loyalists would seem to have been irresistible, for in interpreting the causes of the American Revolution they would seem to have taken over the loyalist line quite directly. The

Revolutionary leaders, Adolphus insisted, were simply "resolute republicans" and their complaints about taxation were flimsy pretenses. They "would not have been satisfied with a total abolition of the claim to taxation"; their aim was revolution and independence from the start; nothing England did would have made any essential difference. The Declaration of Independence, Adolphus declared, was a party screed, abounding in "low and intemperate scurrility," unworthy of an official reply by any agency of the British government, and he recommended to his readers one of the line-by-line refutations of the Declaration that had been published in England "in which every fallacy in argument, every false assumption in principle, every misstatement in fact, was exposed and refuted with so much clearness, perspicuity, and irrefragable force as to render it surprising that a public body should found their defence of an important measure on pretences so fallacious and so extremely open to detection."[6]

But had not the loyalists said the same thing? Had they not in fact written the very replies to the Declaration of Independence that Adolphus found so convincing? Were they not, then, his heroes, and did he not therefore portray their struggles sympathetically and justify them to the world? He did not. He mentions them only to note the embarrassment they caused the British army by the excesses of their zeal and to illustrate the cruelty of their republican enemies. For Adolphus's purpose was to show that the government had acted wisely and humanely throughout. To have justified the loyalists and told their story sympathetically would necessarily have been to see in their warnings early perceptions of the conspiratorial causes of the trouble, and hence to convict king and ministry either of inexcusable deafness to the cries of their most faithful subjects or stupidity in not acting on their warnings before it was too late.[7]

It was not for Adolphus, or for Mahon (who managed to imply that the responsibility for the whole mess lay with the loyalists for not having made their warnings effective),[8] or for any other early-nineteenth-century Tory historian to make sense of the loyalists' opposition to the Revolution, or to show the events through their eyes.[9] Nor was it the appropriate work of the later Whig historians, most notably Trevelyan.

What is in fact remarkable in Trevelyan's treatment of the loyalists is not that he failed to make sense of their opposition to the Revolution, but that he devoted as much sympathetic attention to them as he did.[10] At certain points he depicted their dilemmas sensitively and analyzed skillfully the paralysis these tensions induced. But in the end the loyalists had to be wrong—indeed, stupidly wrong—in choosing to side with the corrupt and reactionary ministry. Naive, provincial dupes of an insensitive and venal government, Trevelyan's loyalists are a pathetic lot, and their lives, as he portrays them, for all their poignancy, make it less rather than more understandable that so foul a regime as that of George III could ever have endured or that anyone but a fool would have supported it.

Thus, for a century the main lines of interpretation either ignored the loyalists or noticed them accusingly to prove a point in what was essentially an argument in English politics. Then suddenly at the end of the nineteenth century the situation was transformed, and a new phase of interpretation began. Books and articles on the loyalists appeared in a rush between 1880 and 1910, in various ways devoted to telling their story sympathetically. The whole balance of the story was shifting and a new structure of interpretation was emerging in which the loyalists would be crucial. Yet this effort was no less partisan than what had gone before. It was simply partisan in a different way, as distorting as that of the previous generation, but rooted in different interests, different needs, different problems.

It was an extraordinary development, this late-nineteenth-century revisionism. It is a revealing example of the intricate way in which American self-identity was shaped by an awareness of England.

It involves some of the most celebrated historians of the time and some of the most obscure and strange. It starts with the magisterial figure of W. E. H. Lecky.

Why Lecky, in his *History of England in the Eighteenth Century,*[11] should have broken out of the existing orthodoxies to reach a breadth of view and a balance of judgment on the leaders of the American Revolution unknown before is not apparent from his published letters or from the *History* itself. It was not simply that he was a thorough and judicious scholar and responded open-mindedly to the wealth of documentation that had become available. The structure of the story was essentially clear in his mind before he saw the hundreds of volumes that are cited in his footnotes. Perhaps his being Irish—in his youth a fervent Irish patriot yet against home rule—helped broaden his view of colonial questions. But for whatever reason, his third and fourth volumes (1882), which cover the Revolution, presented the most carefully balanced assessment of its causes that had yet been seen, and flatly challenged the prevailing pieties.

For Lecky agreed with the Tory view that "the American Revolution, like most others, was the work of an energetic minority, who succeeded in committing an undecided and fluctuating majority to courses for which they had little love, and leading them step by step to a position from which it was impossible to recede." The American people did not want independence; they wanted a redress of grievances, and "it was only very slowly and reluctantly that they became familiarized with the idea of a complete separation from England." And then he wrote, in a passage on the loyalists that is central to his view of the Revolution and that would evoke the most fervent responses in America:

> There were brave and honest men in America who were proud of the great and free Empire to which they belonged, who had no desire to shrink from the burden of maintaining it, who remembered with gratitude all the English blood that had been shed around Quebec and Montreal, and who, with nothing to hope for from the Crown, were prepared to face the most brutal mob violence and the invectives of a scurrilous Press, to risk their fortunes, their reputations, and sometimes even their lives, in order to avert civil war and ultimate separation. Most of them ended their days in poverty and exile, and as the supporters of a beaten cause history has paid but a scanty tribute to their memory, but they comprised some of the best and ablest men America has ever produced, and they were contending for an ideal which was at least as worthy as that for which Washington fought. The maintenance of one free,

industrial, and pacific empire, comprising the whole English race, holding the richest plains of Asia in subjection, blending all that was most venerable in an ancient civilization with the redundant energies of a youthful society, and destined in a few generations to outstrip every competitor and acquire an indisputable ascendancy on the globe, may have been a dream, but it was at least a noble one, and there were Americans who were prepared to make any personal sacrifices rather than assist in destroying it.

Yet despite all the loyalists' idealism, vision, and courage Lecky believed that it was their enemies, the Revolutionary leaders, few in number, antimajoritarian, who in the end had in fact been right. The colonies, he said, were justified in resisting the encroachments of the English state and in refusing to pay taxes that their assemblies had not approved. The example of Ireland, with its "hereditary revenue, the scandalous pension list, the monstrous abuses of patronage," was always before their eyes, "and they were quite resolved not to suffer similar abuses in America." In such men as Samuel Adams, Lecky wrote in a brilliant passage, perfect embodiments of "the fierce and sober type of the seventeenth-century Covenanter . . . poor, simple, ostentatiously austere and indomitably courageous . . . hating with a fierce hatred, monarchy and the English Church, and all privileged classes and all who were invested with dignity and rank"—in such men as these, Lecky wrote, "permeated and indurated" with "the blended influence of Calvinistic theology and of republican principles," the government's impositions could only stir the most explosive reactions.

So it was Adams—fierce, narrow, unbending, ungenerous, intolerant—who had been right. Who then had been wrong? Like Trevelyan, Lecky blamed an insensitive and blundering ministry; but otherwise the breadth of his sympathy seemed limitless. There had been as many heroes and villains on one side of the water, he made clear, as on the other; and if he labored to convince his readers that the victorious Adams contained within his fierce personality the elemental virtues of strength, courage, and an unending devotion to a righteous cause, he declared with equal insistence that the defeated loyalists had had the same virtues, together with perhaps greater vision, and in addition had paid for their convictions with suffering that the triumphant patriots never knew.[12]

This is a remarkably well-balanced judgment; it marks a great advance in interpretation, and it approaches, within the limitations of the knowledge of the time, a rounded perception of the whole. But its great impact on the developing lines of historical understanding in the United States had less to do with the comprehensiveness of Lecky's sympathy than with the pessimistic message that could be derived from his stirring account of the loyalists' superior virtue and vision and their defeat by the likes of Adams. Before the 1880s were out Lecky was being cited again and again by a new group of American writers developing a dark view of the American past that spoke directly to overwhelming problems of their own time and place. For them, Lecky, and through Lecky the loyalists, took on a new and unique importance.

The first of these problems was the question of the ethnic character of American society, a question that obsessed American thinkers at the end of the nineteenth century. Who were the American people? In the course of the 1880s and 1890s nine million immigrants entered the United States. Of the total population of seventy-six million in 1900, over ten million had been born abroad, and almost half of them had come from central, eastern, and southern Europe—peasants in large part, almost totally ignorant of Anglo-American culture. Were all of these people in more than a technical sense equally American? Some—Jeffersonian humanists—never doubted that they were, since they shared the passion for freedom that had motivated the Founding Fathers. Others, anticipating the positive results of a still-emerging process of ethnic mixing, were equally optimistic. But for yet others, of British ancestry and inherited status if not wealth, the immigrant hordes, the frightful slums they seemed to create, the crudeness, violence, and corruption of a new boss-run political system that seemed to violate every principle of a proper democracy—all of this was a threat and a challenge. It evoked elaborate responses and seemed to demand a rethinking of the past.

For as they looked about them at the condition of industrial mass society in America they could only think that the patriotic historians' optimism had been romantic and naive. What struck these writers—amateur historians for the most part, leading figures in the many patriotic, genealogical, and historical societies that were then reaching the height of their importance in the eastern states—what struck them most forcibly was not the relentless march of progress and the broadening amplitudes of freedom but the opposite: the loss of essential qualities that had once created a more agreeable, better-ordered, freer, more comprehensible way of life. Some basic source of integrity must have been destroyed. At some point in the past a profound retrogression must have been set in motion. When and how had it happened? Some men of cosmic vision, broad learning, and imagination—most notably Henry Adams—reached beyond the whole of the modern world and located the source of the decline in such vague and distant events as the destruction of the unity of medieval culture in the twelfth century. But more ordinary American historians turned to their own recent past and found a new meaning in the earliest years of American history and in the Revolution.

What a strange, anxious lot they were, these now obscure but then popular antiquarian scholars, and what romantic things they wrote. Sydney George Fisher, of Philadelphia, for example, a wealthy lawyer and sportsman descended on one side from an original Quaker founder of Pennsylvania and on the other from a Connecticut loyalist: he was obsessed with the menace of the immigrants and wrote article after article with such titles as "Alien Degradation of American Character," "Immigration and Crime," "Has Immigration Dried Up Our Literature?" "Has Immigration Increased Population?"—until at the age of forty he discovered history and found in a peculiar reading of the past an effective leverage over the unpleasantness of his own time which he employed relentlessly through eleven volumes. Many have *"True"* in their titles (*The True Benjamin Franklin, The True History of the American Revolution*), as if everything that had been written before was false and it had been left to him to reveal for the first time the unmythologized, unvarnished, quite miserable truth about where the American people had gone wrong.[13]

Or the more judicious and scholarly land conveyancer, lawyer, and judge, Mellen Chamberlain of Chelsea, Massachusetts, who became a prince, a Borgia, among American autograph collectors, and whose antiquarian and bibliographical interests led eventually to the directorship of the Boston Public Library and to innumerable small, disconnected publications in the *Proceedings of the Massachusetts Historical Society* in which he verified signatures, dated and edited documents, traced ancient land titles, argued about the origins of the New England towns, and memorialized such neglected notables as the loyalist Daniel Leonard.[14]

Or, best of all, the Reverend George E. Ellis, son of a rich Boston merchant and grandson of a loyalist, who quit his Unitarian parish in Charlestown, Massachusetts, in disgust at developments in both church and society and retired to a house on Marlborough Street, Boston, and to the insulating book stacks of the Massachusetts Historical Society, which he served as president for ten years. A dour man (his candid colleagues said in implacably honest tributes to him after his death), who talked in soliloquies or not at all, he had been, they correctly recorded, a "melancholy failure" as professor of theology at the Harvard Divinity School and had repaid Harvard for its lack of response by publicly striking it from the list of beneficiaries in his will. Never known to have uttered a single good word for any reforming cause, never having evinced the slightest interest in art, poetry, fiction, or music, and, on the one occasion in his entire eighty years when he was known to have quoted a phrase from Shakespeare, having quoted it wrong, he "lived in the past," despaired of the future, and worked like a beaver on his antiquarian research and his writing—though he wrote, his candid associates confessed, in a most "cumbrous, clumsy, diffuse" style. The most that could be said for Ellis, it was firmly recorded, was that he was "sober, peaceable, morally clean . . . sensible, and dutiful." And also that he "belonged to the ancient order . . . of privilege."[15]

And that is the essential fact. The history that Ellis, Chamberlain, and Fisher wrote remains significant as an expression of opinion within a group of the highest social status and as a reflection of the challenges they felt. Their writings differ, of course, in quality and emphasis, but they share the same underlying concern, and they agreed that the Revolution, and the role of the loyalists, had been misunderstood.

Fisher hammered away most directly and colorfully at the idea that the Revolution had broken the progressive thread of American history. The pre-Revolutionary period had in truth, he said, been full of arcadian gaiety and bucolic virtue; the people had lived "a glorious life of enjoyment." "It was merry England transported across the Atlantic, and more merry, light, and joyous than England had ever thought of being." Then came the Revolution, which ushered in the money-grubbing culture of a "sullen and depressed" polyglot populace that had no notion of how to amuse itself and furthermore was dominated by elements of the lower classes which in the colonial period had been firmly controlled by the aristocracy. The Revolution, far from having been the "spontaneous, unanimous uprising, all righteousness, perfection, and infallibility" that Americans had been taught to think true, had actually been an unpleasant affair, as full of atrocities, mistakes, and absurdities as any other such upheaval. And the history of the loyalists proved it. The terror they had been forced to endure at the hands of the Revolutionary mobs was doubly revealing, Fisher claimed in detailing their sufferings. It illustrated, first, the essential violence and brutality of the Revolutionary movement, and it marked "the rise of the ignorant classes into power and the steady deterioration in the character and manners of public men."[16]

Conceptually, the loyalists were essential to Fisher's story, and it is not surprising that his most effective piece of writing is an essay in which he reviewed the role of the loyalists in the historiography of the Revolution.[17] It was with them that his sympathies lay. Their plight offered him intellectual control over the social dislocations of his own time, for in his identification with them he found a means of removing himself from the present and associating himself with an original, authentic American tradition from which the present had departed.

So too Ellis, an inner émigré, felt a deep kinship with the loyalists. They had simply been conservatives, and none the worse for that. For the Revolutionary movement, Ellis made clear, had been born in the lawlessness of the radicals and the destructiveness and terrorism of the mobs. As leading conservatives, the loyalists had been "intelligent and excellent persons, who dearly loved their country"; they had been subjected to the worst kinds of abuse simply because they hesitated to join a rebellion. Of what had the loyalists in fact been guilty?

Ellis's ingenious answer—which allowed him to rejoice in his patriotism and exonerate the loyalists at the same time—first appeared in 1884 in a review essay on the first volume of Thomas Hutchinson's *Diary and Letters.* The question, he said, is not one of justice or guilt, but of something quite different: "the fitting time," he wrote in a characteristically meandering metaphor, "had *nearly* come for the colonies to drop away from the mother country by a natural, unaided, unimpeded ripening, as mature fruit drops from the tree. . . . [T]he question left now is whether the process, a little premature, was violently hurried by one party, by pounding and shaking the tree, to anticipate the fruit before it was ripe; or whether the process was blindly and perversely, and also violently, resisted by the other party, in an obstinate refusal to allow the natural and the inevitable." That central and fiercely vilified figure, Hutchinson, he said, was "a man of high integrity, of good judgment, and of noble magnanimity . . . in heart and purpose a true friend of what he believed to be safest and best for his native country." But he had misjudged the ripeness of the fruit. As a native New Englander he should have known, Ellis said, in another of his collapsing agricultural metaphors, "that civil as well as religious independence of the mother country germinated in the first field-planting of the colony, and had been bearing and resowing its own crops, strengthening on their stalks through the generations." In other words, Hutchinson should have known that independence was inevitable and he should have anticipated that as governor "his official duty would require him to dam a current that had already become dangerously swollen."[18]

Four years later Ellis amplified this interpretation of the loyalists. He was now certain that, in the civil war that was called the Revolution, the vast majority of the people had been conservative and loyal until intimidation, or possibly honest conversion, gave the advantage to the patriot leaders. Until crown authority had been destroyed and until the only source of law and order had become Congress or the new state governments, loyalism had been entirely justified, for in essence it was simply "allegiance to established authority as a safeguard against anarchy," and it was heroic in the face of the brutality with which it was met. When the legitimate sources of law changed, the loyalists should have switched sides or silently conformed since by then the only alternative to Congress was anarchy. "They had but to extend the meaning of the term loyalty from its limited reference to the British king to the recognition of Congress, which had established a government."[19]

So the amateurs—Fisher, Chamberlain,[20] Ellis—responded to the tensions of the late nineteenth century by following Lecky and devising an interpretation of the American Revolution that was as much social therapeutics as history and in which the loyalists were respected and important figures. They wrote at a time when modern professional scholarship was evolving rapidly, however, and the purest amalgam of their fervent phil-anglicism was the work of one who linked their antiquarianism to the creative lines of force developing within the universities.

James K. Hosmer was more of a professional historian than his colleagues in the Massachusetts Historical Society, yet he was still a generalist and wide-ranging historical thinker in the manner of Lecky, to whom he acknowledged his deep indebtedness. A Harvard-educated Unitarian minister turned scholar and university teacher, Hosmer sought to present an integrated world view in which history bore directly on the problems of his age. He had the time for such a task (he lived to be ninety-three), and he had the necessary range of interests and skills. Professor at one time or another of history, English literature, German literature, and rhetoric, Hosmer produced a history of the Jews, a history of German literature, four volumes on the American Civil War, a biography of Sir Henry Vane, a *Short History of Anglo-Saxon Freedom,* a biography of Samuel Adams, and a biography (the only one that at that time existed) of Thomas Hutchinson.

Disparate as they were, these books together comprise a general statement—as history, as ideology, and as social commentary. The key work is his *History of Anglo-Saxon Freedom,* which is subtitled "The Polity of the English Speaking Race." Hosmer's purpose was to illustrate "the substantial identity of the great English-speaking nations . . . and the expediency that these nations should, in John Bright's phrase, become one people." The first part of the book flows easily, disposing of everything between 100 B.C. and the settlement of British America in a hundred pages. For the seventeenth and eighteenth centuries the pace slows somewhat, as Hosmer felt it necessary to explain in some detail the ups and downs of freedom under the Stuarts, the Commonwealth, and Walpole's parlia-

mentary system. The great explanatory challenge lay
in the American Revolution, since it had sundered the
English and American people, and he faced it with a
bold fusion of the thought of Lecky and the American antiquarians.

Americans, he wrote, did not fight England in
the Revolution; Americans and Englishmen were
both fighting "the Hanoverian George III and his
Germanized Court," or more generally, English and
American liberals were both fighting autocratic conservatives. Indeed, the two peoples, he declared in a
fine flight of imagination, were interchangeable: if all
the people of England had been transported to America after the Seven Years' War and all the Americans
to England, the same history would have resulted.
To prove this he quoted Lecky for several pages on
the political history of England under George III,
which got him into a muddle trying to keep party
views of the American question consistent.[21] But the
main point is never obscured: America was fighting
to preserve the same liberties for which England had
fought over the centuries. Americans were loyal and
never wished to throw off allegiance to England, and
the loyalists above all were, he said, striving to maintain the unity of the English-speaking peoples. The
loyalists were in fact the superior people "as regards
intelligence, substantial good purpose, and piety."
Their one mistake was to have conceded supremacy to

"distant arbitrary masters," a mistake which "a population nurtured under the influence of the revived
folkmoot ought by no means to have made." This formulation let Hosmer have the argument both ways.
Both the loyalists and their enemies were seeking to
fortify Anglo-Saxonism; the loyalists, however, failed
to see the Anglo-Saxonism of the popular assemblies (the "folkmoots") that opposed them. But that
was the loyalists' only error. Otherwise every human
virtue had been theirs in abundance: grace, chivalry,
courage, poetic spirit, and a generous and dignified
style of life understandably offensive to the coarse
democracy of the town meetings. The strife therefore
was "not of countries but of parties . . . carried on in
each arena for the preservation of the same priceless
treasure,—Anglo-Saxon freedom. . . . What a noble
community is this,—common striving so heroic for
a common cause of such supreme moment! How
mean the nursing of petty prejudice between lands so
linked; how powerful the motive to join hand with
hand and heart with heart!"[22]

Hosmer's two biographies exemplify this theme.
The book on Sir Henry Vane's dual career in England
and Puritan Massachusetts seeks to show the essential
unity of the struggle for freedom among English-
speaking peoples in the seventeenth century, and the
biography of Hutchinson contains the same message
in somewhat different form. It follows perfectly the

theme laid out in *Anglo-Saxon Freedom,* and it follows too the favorable scenario of Hutchinson's life that Hosmer had sketched a decade earlier in his unenthusiastic biography of Samuel Adams. From the opening pages, which quote in full Lecky's view of the loyalists, to Hutchinson's death 350 pages later, the exoneration of this key loyalist from all blame save a single honest error, "disloyalty to the folk-moot," proceeds in heavily documented detail. Hutchinson had been "a sleepless, able captain who went down at last with his ship"; how sad, Hosmer felt, that he did not live to sense if not to witness the recovery that England would make, the strength that America would gain, and the vindication that would be found in both countries for precisely the values that this sensible, destroyed man had held most dear.[23]

The reception of the book is revealing. The reviewer in the *American Historical Review* was a patriot of an earlier vintage, and he filled seven pages with abuse. His attack was aimed partly at Hutchinson for having favored the subjection of the colonies "as mere tributaries of the realm," partly at Hosmer for having attempted to exonerate Hutchinson, with whom, he correctly pointed out, Hosmer had revealed himself to be decidedly more in sympathy than he was with his earlier biographical subject, Adams; and this, he charged, "is a necessary consequence of his concurrence in the new-school views from which we dissent." But one reviewer, Moses Coit Tyler, praised the book enthusiastically: it was "wise, kindly, and patriotic" of Hosmer to have written it, he declared in *The Nation*—words which, Hosmer wrote in a letter of thanks, coming from "the one scholar in America who was best equipped to sit in judgment on such a book as mine, . . . let me know I have succeeded: I really need nothing more."[24]

For Tyler, whose career brings us a step closer to the world of modern professional scholarship, was then emerging as a major figure among American academic historians and one of the leading protagonists of the loyalists. A Connecticut-born descendant of seventeenth-century settlers in New England and a Yale graduate who had become a Calvinist minister, he had spent the Civil War years in Boston doing gymnastics to music under the tutelage of a crusading homeopathic physician, and had taken his muscular Christianity to England. There he had remained as a lecturer on homeopathy and other subjects for three formative years. He had been transfixed by the London of John Bright and Gladstone, of Lord John Russell and Disraeli, and had soaked up what he could of its cultural life. By the time he left, in 1866, he had developed a permanent interest in American history; had referred to the Revolution in his public lectures as "that unlucky quarrel" which would never have happened if the ministry had been well enough informed;

and had been accustomed to use experiences of the loyalists to illustrate what he called in a lecture title "English Hallucinations Touching America."

By the time Lecky's *History of England* appeared, Tyler was professor of American history at Cornell University and the noted author of a two-volume history of American literature covering the years 1607–1765. Lecky's chapters on America gave Tyler immense pleasure. They were, he said, "by their perfect judicial fairness one of the very best means of getting the coming generation of American students out of the old manner of thinking upon and treating American history, which has led to so much Chauvinism among our people." He had long since decided to work to the same goal in a magnum opus on the Revolution that would help overcome the deplorable "race-feud" he believed existed between the two countries as a result of the disruption of the "English-speaking race" at the end of the eighteenth century.

A particularly sympathetic treatment of the loyalists was essential to his purpose in what became *The Literary History of the American Revolution;* and it was not artificially contrived. Tyler loved England; he regretted the Revolution; and he instinctively favored all those who sought the unity of the English-speaking peoples, in the past as in the present. He could only have been deeply grateful to the president of Cornell, a historian himself, who in writing to congratulate him on his book praised him in almost the same terms in which Tyler had praised Lecky—"a marvellous balance"; "marvellous impartiality"—and declared that "the most successful part, . . . the most striking part, is your dealing with the Loyalists. . . . [Y]ou have done the Loyalists full justice," he added, "without going over to their side, as I feared you would do."[25]

But in fact Tyler's book is a series of summaries of the contents of the loyalists' major writings. While it was a significant step forward for him to present the loyalists' writings along with those of the Revolutionary leaders, he had neither the documentation, nor the conceptual grasp, nor the understanding of the context that would allow him to explain properly their side of the origins of the conflict.

Nor indeed did those far more masterful scholars, the so-called imperialist historians, who were young when Tyler was at his height. It was they who carried the phil-anglicism of the nineteenth-century antiquarians directly into the demanding world of academic scholarship.

The distance between the romantic amateurs like Fisher and Ellis, deeply concerned with questions of ethnic identity, and such scholars as George Louis Beer, Herbert L. Osgood, Charles M. Andrews, and Lawrence H. Gipson is vast, but in their original cultural orientation the two groups were in fact close. They were bred in the same culture and shared the same ultimate sources of ideas and attitudes. They all sought to express in historical terms their belief in the kinship of the British and the American peoples; and like Lecky, whom they all admired and quoted, they viewed the Revolution in some degree as unfortunate and the continuing unity of the English-speaking peoples as necessary for survival in a world that was tending, as Lecky prophetically wrote at the end of his life, more and more toward "great political agglomerations based upon an affinity of race, language and creed, which has produced the Pan-Slavonic movement and the Pan-Germanic movement, and which chiefly made the unity of Italy."[26]

In this sense, as intense partisans of the unity of the English-speaking peoples, they were all, emotionally, loyalists. But these modern historians were more concerned with international relations than with domestic social problems, and they were obliged to express their views through the constraints of a large and growing body of historical documentation and in expositions that satisfied the demanding technical requirements of their profession. Andrews devoted most of his many volumes to depicting in one way or another the legal and administrative bonds that had unified England and America before the Revolution. But, like Osgood, who opened his prolific career in the 1890s by urging historians of America not only to work in the British archives but in imagination to station themselves in London in order to "view colonial affairs in their proper perspective," Andrews avoided a detailed account of the revolution that had destroyed the eighteenth-century Anglo-American empire.

Beer too confined his scholarly writing to the pre-Revolutionary period, but his sympathy with the loyalists came out in striking comments in his books and essays, which illustrate dramatically the political relevance of the loyalists for those of a "Pan-Anglian state of mind" in the early years of the twentieth century. He concluded a study in 1907 with the statement that the American Revolution, "in so far as it led to the political disintegration of the Anglo-Saxon race," ran counter to the deepest tendencies of history and that in the future the Revolution may well "lose the great significance that is now attached to it and will appear merely as the temporary separation of two kindred peoples." Ten years later, in a book written during World War I to explain the necessity for "a co-operative democratic alliance of all the English-speaking peoples," Beer developed his earlier conjecture into a flat forecast that ultimately there would be a reunion of the two nations, though he warned against any "premature forcing of the pace."[27]

But it was left to Lawrence Gipson, one of the first American Rhodes Scholars (1904), in his fifteen-volume *British Empire Before the American Revolution* (1936–70), to work out most fully the favorable view of the loyalists consistent with the world that was being created by the "imperialist" historians. The goal of his enormous work was to justify the old British empire against the "terrible indictment" of the Declaration of Independence, and to do so by presenting "a detached, unbiased view of [it] under normal, peace-time conditions."

It is a defensive view, full of nostalgia. Britain's trade acts were not offensive, Gipson wrote, they were made to seem so by colonial smugglers. The Declaratory Act declaring Parliament's supremacy "in all cases whatsoever" was nothing new; it was modeled on the Irish Act of 1719 and had been effectively operative at least since 1696. Responsible people in the colonies did not object to the presence of British troops; such objections were generated by the Sons of Liberty, "these zealots," who deliberately raised in an otherwise inert populace "an ineradicable hatred of the British government," apparently to serve private purposes.

Gipson's warmest sympathies in the volumes on the Revolution are reserved for the loyalists. His first publication, in fact, which appeared sixteen years before the first volume of *The British Empire,* was a sympathetic biography of a loyalist, Jared Ingersoll, of Connecticut; and in the last volumes of the *Empire*

series he continued to adjust the balance of interpretation more in the loyalists' favor. Their plural
officeholding is indulgently explained, their opinions
defended, and their responsibility for the outcome
discounted.[28]

Yet in the end Gipson, though a devoted Anglo-
phile, could hardly say that they had been right and
the Revolution wrong, nor was he able to formulate
the issue in any other terms. It was not possible for
him, given his basically institutional explanation of
historical development, to penetrate into the mental,
psychological, or ideological world of either side. He
wrote of events but not of motivations, of what happened but not of why things happened or of what
people understood was happening. Despite all the
concrete detail of his huge study, the basic forces at
work prove to be impersonal and abstract. The cause
of the Revolution as it emerges from his volumes has
little to do with anyone's specific decisions or actions.
The basic pressure toward what became a revolutionary change came from the development of institutions. The Revolution, as Gipson saw it, was the result
chiefly of the desire of the colonies' lower Houses of
Assembly, which in England were still thought of as
provincial councils possessed of limited and inferior
powers, to gain the autonomy and powers of full
legislative bodies. This difference in viewpoint, he

believed, was irreconcilable, and when the issue was squarely posed in the 1760s a fundamental conflict was inescapable. Gipson expressed this often in the metaphorical terms of children nourished and fostered by an indulgent and somewhat neglectful parent; they grew to political maturity, and in the vigor of early manhood cast off their dependent state.

The interpretation in Gipson's immense work is woven lightly into a detailed narrative fabric. But though it attains a degree of apparent impartiality by relieving both the loyalists and the ministry of much of the blame that had been heaped on them, it does not explain why some people opposed the Revolution; it does not make clear why any sensible person could have failed to associate himself with the unstoppable march forward of the American public institutions that he described.

Gipson's apparent modernity is deceptive. Born in Colorado and educated in Idaho, he had developed his Anglophilia in the three years he spent in Oxford, 1904–7. By the time of his first publication, 1920, doctoral dissertations on technical aspects of the loyalists' lives based on fresh archival research were being written. By 1970, when his fifteenth and final volume in the *British Empire* series was published, the first modern history of the loyalists written by a professional, academic historian had appeared, free of the Anglian sentiment that had inspired Gipson's labors.[29] It would be followed by many other such works, heavily documented, impartial, personally disengaged, associated with large historical themes, but drained of the passions that had once given the subject such profound and controversial relevance.

PART TWO

Peripheries of the
Early British Empire

6

Thomas Hutchinson in Context

The Ordeal Revisited

In recent years, there has been a flood of thorough, celebratory biographies of the Founders of the American nation, and a more remarkable group cannot easily be imagined. They formed one of the most creative circles in modern history. It is hard to know what other group, what other creative circle, to compare them with. And it's hard to know who of this eighteenth-century North American circle—this world-historical junta of public intellectuals and politicians—to single out for preeminence. John Adams, so successful a diplomat and so poor a politician, but always a wonderful human presence, who brooded with penetration on the great issues of his age; or Hamilton, who saw the future of an emerging capitalist world of market economies and helped bring it into being (he was, Talleyrand said, one of the three greatest men of the age, the others being Napoleon and Pitt); or Franklin, that adroit, ingenious, elusive, deliberately self-fashioned icon of Americanism of whom a new biography has been published in each of the past three years; or Madison, whom no biographer can make charming but whom everyone respected in his own time and who is now seen as a world-class constitutional theorist; or Washington, of whom in the past two years we have had two more biographies, and who correctly saw himself as the military creator, then symbol and embodiment, of the first modern republican nation-state.

They were extraordinarily creative men, and indeed none more so than Jefferson—polymath and visionary, but also a tough, successful politician—who enunciated, more brilliantly than anyone else could have done, the glittering ideals of the Revolution while personally mired in the squalor and brutality of slavery.

A remarkable circle of public men, whose accomplishments have been so well known for generations and whose papers—collections of their every recorded utterance—have been published and republished in technically improving editions throughout the twentieth century. We now have the thirty-nine-volume start of the gargantuan multigenerational Adams Papers, and the new and elaborately edited Jefferson, Madison, Franklin, and Hamilton papers. And we have the papers too of others who did not quite reach the highest mark but who were of consequence in the pantheon and whose lives have also been traced in detail: John Dickinson, whose *Farmer's Letters* was the most consequential ideological statement of the early years of the Revolution, who declined to vote for independence but who rose thereafter to positions of respect and authority. And others: Henry Laurens, Robert and Gouverneur Morris, George Mason.

But amid all these triumphant celebrities of our national origins, there was one antihero who was the greatest loser in the Revolution: the last royal governor of Massachusetts, Thomas Hutchinson. To Adams and the entire New England political intelligentsia he was not only, as the region's leading crown officer, a natural political opponent but also the most villainous, traitorous person in the land. He had betrayed his country to the autocrats of Britain; he personified, they believed, all the corruption and the incipient tyranny that they were fighting against.

Yet as the monumental biographies of the Founders were being written and the scholarly editions of their papers were being prepared, it was Hutchinson's biography I chose to write, and I did so for two reasons that were compelling to me.

First, I found the bitter, vicious vilification of Hutchinson by the Founders to be mysterious, unaccountable. It baffled me, and I wanted to explain it. For no one loved his native land more than Hutchinson. His small property in Milton, Massachusetts, was, he said over and over, to him the most precious spot on earth. No one had deeper roots in the land than this fifth-generation New Englander, whose great-great-grandmother Anne had been one of the major figures in the first years of the Puritans' settlement—long before the Adams, Otis, and Hancock families had been heard of—and whose merchant forebears had been among the originators of the region's Atlantic commerce. He was remarkably accomplished. No American, North or South, wrote better history than he, nor had a more sophisticated, historicist sense of what the study of the past is all about. When in his exile in England Hutchinson was told by the famous Scottish historian William Robertson that he had refused to write the history of the English colonies because "there was no knowing what would be the future condition of them," Hutchinson replied that "be it what it may, it need make no odds in writing the history of what is past, and I thought a true state of them ought to be handed down to posterity."[1]

Adams, his worst enemy, confessed that Hutchinson "understood the subject of coin and commerce better than any man I ever knew in this country," and Hutchinson had joined with Franklin in drafting the first plans for a colonial union. Though technically untrained in the law ("I never presumed to call myself a lawyer. The most I could pretend to was, when I heard the law laid down on both sides, to judge which was right"), Hutchinson proved to be a judicious and efficient chief justice of the Superior Court.[2] In politics he was active, bold, and forthright, but never a mean-spirited, vituperative, vengeful antagonist; his speeches, memos, letters, and formal pronouncements were logical, rational, cool, and cogent. His aim in politics was to keep the peace, maintain the received structure of authority, and enforce the law in accepted, traditional ways. The Puritan virtues of self-restraint, personal morality, worldly asceticism, and, above all, stubborn insistence on pursuing the truth however unpopular or dangerous it might be to do so were essential parts of his personality. He was acquisitive, but not ostentatious; eager for public office—for his family as much as for himself—but careful not to overstep the accepted bounds of law and custom. Though more dutiful than colorful and in appearance unimpressive—a contemporary described him as "tall, thin, half-starved"[3]—he was intelligent, well-informed, well educated, and capable of clear exposition, with a writer's instinct to resolve and objectify his experience by writing about it, if not with Jefferson's lyrical flow then with Madison's concision and accuracy of phrasing. In this sense his life was surprisingly contemplative. And the more I saw of his voluminous writings—his huge correspondence, his three-volume history of Massachusetts, his state papers, and his extraordinary bifocal set piece, the dramatic dialogue between an American and a European Englishman, which he wrote in 1768 but never published—the more I saw of all this, the more impressed I was with his ability and the deeper the mystery of his rejection and the hatred he inspired.

But there was a second reason for undertaking the biography. When I began work on *The Ordeal of Thomas Hutchinson* we were approaching the bicentennial of independence and were distant enough from the event to view the whole of it, not foreshortened to anticipate an inevitably triumphant outcome. One could now see, I believed, the full context of the time, the contingencies and accidents, and understand the circumstances that constrained all involved, winners and losers, the boundaries that shaped all their lives. One could grasp, as I wrote then, the tragedy of it all—tragedy not in the sense of sad misfortune or of the disastrous consequences of hubris, but in the sense of limitations that bound all the actors. We were in a position to recover the uncertainties of the people of the time, who, unlike ourselves, did not know what their future would be—for whom, therefore, risk-taking was the key to everything they did.

I could think of no better way of withholding the outcome of history—of recovering the indeterminacies of that distant time—than to study the losers impartially, even sympathetically, to consider that they had been people who, if things had gone differently, might have emerged as victors. This is not to say that the losers were more worthy of victory than the winners. It is only a way of approaching the past as it actually was: unpredictable, full of clashes of personalities and interests that had no certain futures, a world like our own, alive with possibilities, none of which, in the contingencies of the time, could have been predicted to succeed.

Nothing was inevitable. The American Revolution was not inevitable. Could Hutchinson have kept a lid on the resistance in Boston and prevented it from exploding as it did? The answer is yes. The situation in Boston was inflamed but more or less stable as late as 1771–72, when Hutchinson asked to be relieved of his governorship, which he had been reluctant to accept in the first place, and allowed to retire with dignity. And even in the tea crisis in December 1773 he might have saved the situation by ignoring the law, allowing the tea ships to depart without unloading, thus illegally but prudently preventing an irreversible escalation of conflict. And could Britain have won the military conflict? Again, yes. As late as 1777, after two and a half years of open conflict, America was still fighting a largely defensive war, and British victory was still the reasonable outcome, until the battle of Saratoga in October of that year—and the outcome of that engagement could not have been predicted.

My purpose in studying Hutchinson, then, was partly to explain the anomaly of his evident ability and patriotism on the one hand and the hatred he evoked on the other, and partly to recover through studying his ordeal something of the uncertainties, the contingencies of the time, the deeper context, the unpredictability. Having previously explored at length the world view of the victors, the triumphant ideology that we inherit from them, I hoped to look at the same transforming events from the other side, the side of the losers, whose most articulate native spokesman was Thomas Hutchinson.

So, in 1974 *The Ordeal of Thomas Hutchinson* was published. The reactions were interesting, though I have to say a little disconcerting. Some American reviewers liked it, but others, as I had anticipated, said that this biography of a law-and-order conservative who struggled against popular mobs and protestors could only be a disguised defense of Richard Nixon. Still others said that in various ways I had got it wrong. Some British reviewers were kinder. Lord Blake said it was "one of the outstanding political biographies of modern times," a remark that warmed my heart, until I recalled that among historians Robert Blake was a leading Tory. And J. H. Plumb said it was "a work of art," which was something to put on one's gravestone, though I had to keep in mind that Plumb had sponsored the Trevelyan Lectures in the University of Cambridge which were the basis of the book, and that though liberal in many ways, he was a friend of royalty and a brilliant narrator of their lives and times. Though the book won an award, it soon fell into obscurity, to be occasionally referred to as dubious if not mistaken on particular points by subsequent biographers of Hutchinson.[4]

But it was this book that I thought I would go back to when I received the American Antiquarian Society's kind invitation to deliver the first of the Baron Lectures, a series to be devoted to retrospective views of an author's earlier work, "describing the genesis of and response to it and reflecting on it in the current context of scholarship." I did so because the reasons that had led me to write the book in the first place were not only still compelling in my mind but had become even more relevant in view of the flood of celebratory books on the Founders and the great expansion of our knowledge of eighteenth-century history.

Knowing more now about the greater eighteenth-century world than I did when I wrote the book and understanding the lives and thought of the Founders in greater detail, I now find the context of Hutchinson's life more complex than I did before and his ordeal more revealing of the forces at work in the world at large in the late eighteenth century. I am more certain now that it was Hutchinson, of all the American writers of the time, who best understood the established wisdom, the rock-solid, sanctified truth in matters of politics and political thought as it was then known.

It was he who saw most clearly the apparent flaws in the Founders' arguments and did his best to convince them that what they were arguing was illogical, misguided, and certain to lead to disaster. That in the long run he was wrong is beside the point. At the time no one could have confidently predicted that. What he wrote and what he argued with increasing passion and ultimately despair was accurate, rational, and more logical than what his opponents staked their lives on. No crown official in America, or indeed in Britain, argued the government's case more fully and more clearly than this dutiful provincial.

And no one besides Hutchinson in the whole of colonial officialdom could have sustained the elaborate, learned public debate on constitutional principles he held in 1773 with the Massachusetts Assembly led by John Adams and James Bowdoin.

At the heart of that remarkable series of exchanges, now republished with scholarly commentary as *The Briefs of the American Revolution,* and in Hutchinson's other speeches and papers, lay an inverted relationship between power and liberty.[5] Hutchinson argued that Britain's *power,* expressed by Parliament, logically, systematically, and necessarily extended to its colonies, but that its *liberties,* in their entirety, did not. His opponents argued precisely the opposite: that Parliament's power did not extend to its dominions, but that English liberties did. They were as valid in America as in the realm of England itself.

This great problem—of the boundaries and location of power and liberty—was the central constitutional struggle of the developing revolution, and no one defined it more clearly than Hutchinson.

As to power, he explained again and again, there could be no limit to the absolute authority of the King-in-Parliament. The Declaratory Act of 1766 asserting Parliament's "full power and authority . . . to bind the colonies in all cases whatsoever" was a statement not of political choice but of logical necessity. For absolute and final power, he wrote, is the defining characteristic of any sovereign entity; it could not be shared without being destroyed. In its nature—by definition—it was indivisible. While Parliament *would* not use its power arbitrarily and unjustly, there was nothing to prevent it from doing so. Whatever it did was constitutional since the King-in-Parliament and all its enactments, together with the common law, *were* the constitution. If Parliament erred, it would, for its own good if for no other reason, correct its error, as it did in repealing the Stamp Act. The colonists' groping and failing efforts to set out limits to Parliament's power—by rejecting its taxing power while accepting its legislative power or by claiming that the colonial assemblies had exclusive powers of their own and yet were loyal to Britain through the crown—none of this made sense, Hutchinson argued, for sovereign power was exclusive and indivisible.

Was he wrong? By 1776 the rebellious leaders themselves realized that their efforts to share sovereignty with Parliament had failed. If Britain insisted that Parliament's power was either exclusive and absolute or nothing, they would choose nothing, thus precisely enacting Edmund Burke's prediction in his speech on American taxation in 1774:

> If, intemperately, unwisely, fatally, you sophisticate and poison the very source of government, by urging subtle deductions, and consequences odious to those you govern, from the unlimited and illimitable nature of supreme sovereignty, you will teach them . . . to call that sovereignty itself in question. When you drive him hard, the boar will surely turn upon the hunters. If that sovereignty and their freedom cannot be reconciled, which will they take? They will cast your sovereignty in your face. No body will be argued into slavery.[6]

Later, in 1787, the Founders returned to the problem in setting up a federalist structure for the national government, a sharing of power between the national and state governments, which we inherit. But while the federalism they invented assigned significant powers to the states, in the end the national government had, as it has, ultimate sovereignty—a fundamental fact of American constitutionalism mandated not by the Founders in 1787, who for political reasons had not dared to write absolute national supremacy into the Constitution, but by successive federal judges who saw the inescapable logic of state formation. Two hundred years later, Max Weber, analyzing theoretically the logical structures of political authority, explained that "a state is a human community that (successfully) claims the monopoly of the legitimate use of physical force within a given territory . . . . The state is considered the sole source of the 'right' to use violence." Hutchinson had written that "it is essential to the being of government that a power should always exist which no other power within such government can have right to withstand or controul."[7] Yet for his insistence on the logic of sovereign power Hutchinson was vilified, charged with denying his fellow colonists the rights that were theirs.

But that was a minor charge next to the firestorm of condemnation that fell on him when his views on liberties, written in private letters of 1767–69, were revealed to the public in 1773. That blistering and defining episode, from which Hutchinson's reputation never recovered, was provoked by Franklin, who obtained the letters in London from an unknown source and then sent them to Boston with instructions to restrict their circulation to a designated few. He knew that they would eventually be published and hoped that they would divert the blame for Britain's repressive actions from the ministry to a few "very mischievous men" in Boston, led by Hutchinson, who, Franklin and the Boston leaders would claim, had misrepresented the colonies as a community in continuous turmoil, defiant of all law and order and determined to throw off allegiance to Britain. But if that was Franklin's plan, it succeeded only in part—not in creating a window for conciliation between America and Britain but in destroying Hutchinson's career and in the process elevating Franklin himself to the status of a patriot hero in America. For what the letters revealed was that in 1768–69 Hutchinson had written privately to a correspondent in England that it was impossible for "a colony 3,000 miles distant from the parent state [to] enjoy all the liberty of the parent state"—that it was simply a matter of fact that there would have to be "an abridgement of what are called English liberties" in America if the tie to Britain were to be retained; and if that tie were lost, the defenseless colonies would be vulnerable to all the predatory powers at work in the world of warring nations and all English liberties would then be lost.[8]

Once those words were published, the entire colonial world, it seemed, exploded in wrath. The New

England newspapers boiled with rage at this betrayal of freedom by "vipers whose poison has already destroyed the health of your province and spilt the blood of your people." John Adams was outraged by this "vile serpent . . . bone of our bone, born and educated among us." His call for an abridgement of English liberties was so flagrant, so Machiavellian a treason, Adams wrote, that "it bore the evident mark *of* madness . . . his reason was manifestly overpowered." The indignation spread as the letters were published and republished locally, then splashed across the newspapers in almost every colony in America. Hutchinson was burned in effigy in Philadelphia and Princeton, and compared to Cataline, Caligula, and Nero.[9]

But what had Hutchinson actually written? Again and again, in letters to everyone he could reach, he explained that he had never said or implied that he *hoped* that English liberties would be restricted, that he had *wished* it, only that it was a matter of logic and observable fact that the colonies' removal from the homeland *must* create an abridgement of liberties—"must" in a descriptive, not volitional sense—it could not be otherwise. "I did not see how it could be helped," he said again and again. As to the "secrecy" of these comments, there was nothing secretive about them. Had he not, in a speech to the Assembly a year earlier, said exactly the same thing? "It is impossible," he had then so publicly said, that "the rights of English subjects should be the same in every respect in all parts of the dominions"—and no one had read treason into that statement then. The furor had been cooked up by the process by which the letters had been revealed, as if it had been the discovery of some deep-lying conspiracy to destroy the colonists' liberties.[10]

There is something poignant in this crisis in Hutchinson's career—poignant because the words that had been revealed so dramatically touched on a profound reality he sensed but did not, or could not, fully explain. What was it about the removal of Englishmen to distant lands that would necessitate an abridgement, a modification of liberties? The one explanation he offered was the fact that while Englishmen (at least some of them) participated in the election of those who ruled them, and who presumably shared their interests, Americans did not. But he implied much more than that. The entire constitutional system, he seemed to be suggesting, was somehow involved. Two hundred years later, legal scholars would be able to explain more fully the deeper basis of Hutchinson's argument.

There is a profound difference, modern historians of English law write, between, on the one hand, the common law as jurisdictional: that is, a system "inseparable from the institutions that applied, practiced, and taught the common law—the Westminster courts, their circuits, the common law bar, and the Inns of Court"—and, on the other hand, the law as jurisprudential: that is, "a rationally organized body of rules and principles defined primarily in reference to each other not to the remedies and personnel enforcing them." In the writings of the seventeenth-century authorities that Hutchinson relied on—above all the great jurist Lord Coke—the common law was conceived of in primarily jurisdictional not jurisprudential terms, that is, as the "craft wisdom" of a particular court system that served it, and that jurisdictional system was bound to its natural roots in the realm of England and not its external dominions. While the crown had jurisdiction over all its dominions, Coke had explained, the common-law courts did not. In Coke's eyes, "English liberties did not follow Englishmen abroad." They went no farther than the English border. "[Coke] never envisioned the common law," a legal historian has recently written, "as a free-floating jurisprudence that could be invoked as a shield against royal administration." Hutchinson conceived of the common law as Coke had done, "as a system of licenses to sue in territorially bounded courts," not as his opponents did, as "an abstract jurisprudence operative in all of the crown's dominions." In this, which was construed by local patriots such as

Adams as treason, Hutchinson was a better lawyer and a better historian than his opponents, but a far poorer politician.[11]

He was right too—this bland provincial official—in other ways. In his remarkable unpublished "Dialogue between an American and a European Englishman," a wide-ranging exploration not only of the great public issues dividing England and America but of universal principles of governance and allegiance, he insisted that the law is not, as his opponents seemed to think, a moral code. The relation between law and morality, he wrote, was subtle and fluid. To sacrifice law for some abstract moral good, however worthy, would in the end destroy all law and with it the foundation of civilized society. But is not civil disobedience justifiable *morally,* the American Englishman asks? Yes, the European replies, but *only* morally. The rebel may be right *morally,* but the moral basis for his actions can never be recognized by the courts. And then followed this striking passage, which Hutchinson wrote and rewrote in successive drafts with great care for every word:

> every individual must take the consequence of a mistake if he attempts to stir up the body of a people to a revolt and should be disappointed. In a moral view he may perhaps be innocent whether his attempt succeeds or not, but . . . as

a member of the political body . . . he must be pronounced guilty by the judiciary powers of that society if he fails of success. This is a principle essential to the nature of government and to the English constitution as well as all others.[12]

No contemporary American lawyer, no political thinker until jurists such as James Wilson and John Marshall, would penetrate more deeply into such root issues of constituted authority.

At the end of the book I attempted to sum up the meaning of Hutchinson's ordeal. Perhaps I may be forgiven now if I repeat what I then wrote:

> Failing to respond to the moral indignation and the meliorist aspirations that lay behind the protests of the Revolutionary leaders, Hutchinson could find only persistent irrationality in their arguments, and he wrote off their agitations as politically pathological. And in a limited, logical sense he was right. The Revolutionary leaders were not striving to act reasonably or logically. Demanding a responsiveness in government that exceeded the traditional expectations of the time, groping towards goals and impelled by aspirations

that were no recognized part of the world as it was, they drew on convictions more powerful than logic and mobilized sources of political and social energy that burst the boundaries of received political wisdom. Hutchinson could not govern an aroused populace led by politicians manipulating deep-felt ideological symbols. He could not assimilate these new forces into the old world he knew so well, and attempting uncomprehendingly to do so, lost the advantage of his greatest assets: a deserved reputation for candor, honesty, and a tireless and impartial devotion to the general good. Failing to carry the new politics with him by arguments that were accredited and tactics that were familiar, he . . . appeared hypocritical, ultimately conspiratorial, though in fact he was neither. As the pressure mounted, his responses narrowed, his ideas became progressively more limited, until in the end he could only plead for civil order as an absolute end in itself, which not only ignored the explosive issues but appeared, unavoidably, to be self-serving.[13]

This was my conclusion when I wrote the book. How does it strike me now? Reasonable, I'm relieved to say, but it is too narrow a judgment. The context is too limited. There is a much larger history of which Hutchinson's ordeal is a part, a broader context in which to locate his efforts, achievements, and failure.

The stirrings in North America in which Hutchinson was so fatally ensnared and which would result in the independence of the coastal North American colonies were part of much greater movements. They were local manifestations of shifts in deep-lying cultural tectonics that undermined the foundations of the whole of Atlantic civilization and led to profound transformations.

The year 1776, when Hutchinson received an honorary degree at Oxford (which happened in fact on the Fourth of July), saw the publication of Tom Paine's *Common Sense,* that flaming indictment of the whole structure of the British monarchy and aristocracy; the publication too of the first volume of Gibbon's *Decline and Fall of the Roman Empire,* that so ironically slighted the established pieties of complacent churchmen; of Richard Price's *Observations on the Nature of Civil Liberty,* that probed the inner nature of political liberty and proposed a Congress of Europe; of Adam Smith's *Wealth of Nations,* that argued for the demolition of commercial regulations and the release of personal self-interest; and of Jeremy Bentham's *Fragment on Government,* that aimed to overthrow the principles of the British constitution and that introduced the radical concept of utilitarianism.

The year of American independence was thus a year of challenges in every sphere of British life—in ideology, politics, religion, economics, law, and the principles of international relations—but not only British life. The entire Western world felt similar tremors that would lead within a single generation to widespread transformations.

The ideas of the Enlightenment, the maturing of colonial societies, and the emergence of industrial economies were eroding the foundations not only of Europe's *ancien régime* but of the Western Hemisphere's establishments as well. While the Latin American independence movements would erupt only after Napoleon's invasion of Spain in 1808, resistance to Spain's Bourbon reforms, parallel to Britain's colonial reforms after the Seven Years' War, provoked patriotic aspirations among the Spanish American Creole elite and demands for home rule within an imperial commonwealth and representation in a central Hispanic Cortes. At the same time popular uprisings of the indigenous, African, and mixed-race populations erupted everywhere: in Peru, in the rebellion led by Túpac Amaru in 1780; in Colombia, in the Comunero Revolution of 1781; in Saint-Domingue, in the bloody insurrection of 1794 that convulsed the entire colonial world with scenes of plantation massacres and the threat of emancipation; and in Mexico, in the insurgency led by Diego Hidalgo and José Maria

Morélos in 1810, inspired by a passion for ethnic equality.

There were shifting winds everywhere, from Paris to Cádiz, from the Netherlands to Peru, from Boston to Ecuador. The structure of the Atlantic world, which had developed over three centuries, seemed to be crumbling. In this vast panorama of challenges and transformations the helplessness of Thomas Hutchinson—this thoughtful, rational, logical, well-informed provincial official clinging so conscientiously to traditional verities while the world around him pitched and churned—is a vivid symbol and a revealing symptom of the tumult of the age. Seen through his eyes it was not the exhilarating, creative beginning of a new, modern world but a painful evanescence and loss of certainty. He knew that logic and experience were on his side, but he had no way of grasping, in the apparent irrationality of his opponents' views, the forces of innovation that would remake the Atlantic world. He could only insist—sensibly, logically, and fatally—that "we don't live in Plato's Commonwealth, and when we can't have perfection we ought to comply with the measure that is least remote from it." So he was, as he said himself, "a quietist, being convinced that what is, is best."[14]

In his defeat and bewilderment one finds the full measure of the Founders' creativity, for to overcome

the authority of Hutchinson's convictions, which dis-
tilled the wisdom of the ages, took nothing less than
the recasting of the basic structure of established
constitutional and political thought. They did not
succeed all at once or completely, nor did Hutchinson's beliefs immediately disappear. But the Founders sensed the motion of the changing cultural tides
bearing improvement if not perfection, and propelled
it forward. In their world independence was an erup-
tive triumph, to be celebrated, Adams so famously
wrote, "as the day of deliverance . . . with pomp and
parade, with shows, games, sports, guns, bells, bon-
fires and illuminations, from one end of this continent
to the other from this time forward forever more."[15]
In Hutchinson's world the honor bestowed on him by
Oxford on the Fourth of July could not compensate
for the alienation and bewilderment he felt, nor the
belittlement he would endure in the years of exile
that followed as he stood alone, day after day, at the
king's receptions, gray and gaunt, silently beseeching.

7

England's Cultural Provinces

Scotland and America

The question of the origin of the "Scottish Renaissance"—that remarkable efflorescence of the mid-eighteenth century, with its roll call of great names: Hume, Smith, Robertson, Kames, and Ferguson—is one of those historical problems which have hitherto stubbornly resisted a definite solution. This may be due to its very nature; for, as the greatest of recent historians of Scotland has remarked, "We recognize as inadequate all attempts to explain the appearance of galaxies of genius at particular epochs in different countries."[1] This is not to imply that attempted explanations have failed to be forthcoming. On the contrary, ever since a learned Italian named Carlo Deanina applied himself to the problem in *An Essay on the Progress of Learning among the Scots* (1763), historians have suggested different reasons for that striking and apparently sudden outburst of creative energy. Macaulay saw the principal cause for what he considered "this wonderful change" from the barren wastes of seventeenth-century theology in the act passed by the Estates of Scotland in 1696, setting up a school in every parish. His contemporary Henry Buckle, sounding a suitably Darwinian note, observed that the energies displayed in the Scottish political and religious struggles of the seventeenth century had survived those struggles to find another field in which they could exert themselves.

There is something to be said for both these points of view. The national system of education, though in practice never quite as ideal as in conception, enabled many a poor farmer's boy to go on to one of the universities as well prepared as his socially superior classmates. Nor can it be denied that in spite of the Jacobite rebellions of 1715 and 1745 the general atmosphere of eighteenth-century Scotland was more conducive to peaceful pursuits than that of the strife-torn decades of the seventeenth century. But it requires no more than a little reflection on cultural history to perceive that neither peace nor public education, nor their conjunction, guarantees the intellectual achievements suggested by the word "renaissance."

Similar objections may be advanced concerning some of the other so-called causes of Scotland's golden age. Thus it is certainly true that the eighteenth century, in contrast to the seventeenth, was for Scotland a period of increasing economic prosperity. However, the disastrous Darien scheme of the 1690s ate up that capital fuel without which even the most rigorous

Protestant ethic could not become economically effi-
cacious. The immediate effect of the Union of 1707
was not the expected sudden prosperity, but increased
taxation and loss of French trade. Nor, until much
later, was there a compensating expansion of commerce with England and the colonies. Real economic
advancement did not come until the latter half of the
century, too late to serve as a satisfactory reason for
the first stages of Scotland's great creative period. As
for the influence of "New Light" Francis Hutcheson,
his Glasgow lectures—effusions on the marvelous
powers of the "moral sense"—no doubt "contributed
very powerfully to diffuse, in Scotland, that taste for
analytical discussion, and that spirit of liberal inquiry,
to which the world is indebted for some of the most
valuable productions of the eighteenth century."[2]
But holding them solely responsible for the Scottish
Enlightenment is surely expecting a little too much
even from the most lucid philosopher. Furthermore,
it is worth noting that after Hutcheson's first year
at Glasgow, at least one contemporary observer sin-
gled him out for praise because he was maintaining
the cause of orthodox Christianity in a university
shot through with free thought.[3] The fact is that by
the time Hutcheson began his lectures, considerable
breaches had been made in the dam of orthodox aus-
terity so laboriously constructed during the embattled
decades of the previous century.

Adequate explanation of the origins of the Scottish Renaissance, therefore, must take account not only of a variety of social factors at the moment of fullest flowering, but also of the conditions of growth in the preceding period.[4] Thus broadened, the problem seems to involve the entire history of Scotland for the better part of a century. The numerous elements that entered into the renaissance must be brought together. But the interpretation of broad historical movements of this kind is not simply a matter of listing factors. A knowledge of their configuration is equally important. Comprehension of Scotland's renaissance must rest on an appreciation of the essential spirit of the time and place, as well as on the accumulation of cultural data.

The underlying unity of this renaissance, the profound impulses that elevated the life of a nation, require deeper study and thought than they have yet received. We do not propose to solve such problems in these few pages. We seek, merely, possible perspectives within which to perceive them. For the American colonies too enjoyed a flowering in the eighteenth century—not a renaissance, but yet a blossoming worthy of the designation "golden age." British North America produced no Hume or Adam Smith, but in Edwards and Franklin, Jefferson, Madison, and Adams, Rittenhouse, Rush, Copley, West, Wythe, and Hutchinson it boasted men of impressive accomplishment. Its finest fruit, the literature of the American Revolution, has justly been called "the most magnificent irruption of the American genius into print."[5]

The society in which the achievements of these men were rooted, though obviously different from that of Scotland in many ways, was yet significantly related to it. Elements of this relationship struck contemporaries much as they have later scholars. "Boston," writes one critic, "has often been called the most English of American cities, but in the eighteenth and early nineteenth centuries it was a good deal more like Edinburgh than like London. . . . The people, like those of Edinburgh, were independent, not easily controlled, assertive of their rights."[6] In Boston, New York, and Philadelphia, as in Edinburgh and Glasgow, private clubs, where pompous, often ridiculously elaborate ritual threw into bold relief the fervor of cultural uplift, were vital social institutions. Similar to the quality of social mobility that led Dr. Alexander Hamilton to berate New York's "aggrandized upstarts" for lacking "the capacity to observe the different ranks of men in polite nations or to know what it is that really constitutes that difference of degrees" was the spirit of "shocking familiarity" in Scotland of which Boswell, on his Continental tour, took care to warn Rousseau.[7]

Such remarks tell much and suggest more. They

lead one to pursue the question of the social similarities bearing on intellectual life into richer, if more remote regions. They suggest the value of a comparison of the cultural developments in Scotland and America from the standpoint of the English observer in London. Certain common social characteristics of these flowerings, thus isolated, might throw new light on the basic impulses of the Scottish Renaissance and prove of interest to historians of both regions.

We find, first, a striking similarity in the social location of the groups that led the cultural developments in the two areas.

Whatever else may remain obscure about the social history of colonial America, it cannot be doubted that advance in letters and in the arts was involved with social ascent by groups whose status in Europe would unquestionably have been considered inferior or middling. Despite the familial piety that has so often claimed nobility for *arrivé* forebears, and with it a leisured, graceful intimacy with the muses, there were few cultivated aristocrats in the colonies to lead intellectual and artistic advances. Throughout the North, the middle-class origins of the literati were unmistakable.

Who led the cultural advance in the northern towns? Ministers, of course, like William Smith, provost of the College of Philadelphia, who carried with him from Aberdeen not only a headful of learning but frustrated ambitions that developed into a common type of cultural snobbery; like Samuel Johnson, president of King's College, who grew up in Connecticut, where, he wrote in his poignant *Autobiography,* "the condition of learning (as well as everything else) was very low," and whose "thirst after knowledge and truth" alone saved him from a hopeless provincialism; or like the supercilious Mather Byles, scion of a local intellectual dynasty, who snapped the whip of sarcasm over a mulish populace while proudly displaying a note from Alexander Pope elicited by fawning letters and gifts of hackneyed verse.[8]

Equally important were lawyers like John Adams, William Livingston, and James DeLancey, whose cultural even more than political ascendancy was assured "in a Country," Cadwallader Colden wrote in 1765, "where few men except in the profession of the Law, have any kind of literature, where the most opulent families in our own memory, have arisen from the lowest rank of people."[9] Along with these two professional groups, there were a few of the leading merchants, or, more frequently, their more leisured heirs, like the versifier Peter Oliver or his politician-historian cousin Thomas Hutchinson. These men, potentates on the local scene, were no more than colonial businessmen in the wider world of British society. Even the brilliant classicist and scientist James Logan of Philadelphia—"aristocrat" by common historical designation—would have been but a cultivated Quaker burgher to the patrons of arts and letters in London.

If such were the leaders in the northern port towns, who followed? The numerous cultural associations, the clubs, were recruited from the professional middle and tradesman lower middle classes. Franklin's famous Junto was a self-improvement society of autodidacts. Its original membership included a glazier, a surveyor, a shoemaker, a joiner, a merchant, three printers, and a clerk. And though Philadelphia's merchants derided the Junto as the "Leather Apron Club," they themselves, in their own societies, like their fellows in Annapolis's Tuesday Club, or Newport's Literary and Philosophical Society, could not help finding relaxation in most unaristocratic self-improvement.

But it is of course in the South where the brightest image of the aristocrat, the landed gentleman as the man of letters, has appeared. Wealth in land and slaves, we have been told again and again, combined to create a class of leisured aristocrats—the Byrds, the Carters, the Lees—whose lives glowed with vitality in letters as in politics. But careful study has shown this to be a myth. "The most significant feature of the Chesapeake aristocracy," writes Carl Bridenbaugh,

> was its middle-class origin. . . . Leisure was a myth; endless work was a reality quite as

much for successful planter-gentlemen as for their lesser confreres—and the same held for their womenfolk as well. . . . Those who have appointed themselves custodians of the historical reputation of this fascinating region have generally insisted that it produced that which, by its very nature, it could not produce—a developed intellectual and artistic culture rivaling that of any other part of the colonies. . . . They led a gracious but not a cultured life. . . . The Chesapeake society produced a unique bourgeois aristocracy with more than its share of great and noble men; they were, however, men of intellect, not intellectuals.[10]

What of the deeper South—the society of colonial Carolina? "Families of actual gentle birth were even fewer [here] than in the Chesapeake country; the bourgeois grown rich and seeking gentility set the style. . . . The striking aspects of colonial Charles Town were the absence of cultural discipline and the passiveness of the city's intellectual and artistic life." If Carolina's rising merchant-planter families produced "the only leisure-class Society of colonial America" where alone "enjoyment, charm, refinement—became the *summum bonum*," they yet failed to furnish even a few recruits to the arts and sciences.[11]

How sharp is the contrast to Scotland, with its ancient landed families and tighter social organization?

It would be wrong to ignore the share of the aristocracy in the cultural life of eighteenth-century Edinburgh; but, due to special circumstances, its role remained contributory rather than decisive. The Scottish nobility and gentry had largely remained Jacobite and Episcopalian, even after the reestablishment of the Church of Scotland. This meant that they were unencumbered by those ascetic proclivities against which even moderate Presbyterians still had to struggle. Too poor to travel abroad, they spent their winters in what was no longer the political but still the legal and ecclesiastical capital, where they wrote and sang ballads, sponsored assemblies and diverse entertainments—fostered, in short, an atmosphere of ease and social grace. But if they were masters of the revels, they were masters of little else. While Jacobitism kept conscientious younger sons out of professions requiring an oath to the House of Hanover, poverty forced many of them to earn their living as tradesmen. "Silversmiths, clothiers, woollen drapers were frequently men of high birth and social position."[12] Economic necessity of this sort helped to create in the Old Town of Edinburgh a society in which social demarcations were far from sharply drawn, in which status was as much a function of professional achievement as of birth. Thus Peter Williamson's first *Edinburgh Directory* (1773–74), listing citizens in order of rank, was headed by the Lords of Session, Advocates, Writers to the Signet, and Lords' and Advocates' Clerks. The category of "noblemen and gentlemen" followed after.[13]

This order of precedence was symptomatic of the fact that in the course of the century, social and cultural leadership had fallen to the professional classes, and especially to the legal profession. A good example of the close connection between law and letters is provided by an analysis of the membership of the Select Society, founded in 1754 for the dual purpose of philosophical inquiry and improvement in public speaking. By 1759, this society (then numbering 133 members) had come to include all the Edinburgh literati; and out of 119 who can be readily identified by profession, at least 48 were associated with the law in one way or the other.[14] Along with university professors and members of the Moderate party among the clergy, it was the lawyers who played the principal role both in the mid-eighteenth- and early-nineteenth-century stages of the Scottish Enlightenment. That Scotland retained its own legal system after the Union, that the law thus became the main ladder for public advancement, and that there prevailed a great interest in legal studies had other less direct though no less important consequences. The traditionally close involvement of

Scottish and Roman law, as well as the liberal influences brought home from Holland by generations of Scottish law students at Utrecht and Leiden, proved to be forces conducive to fresh currents of philosophical and historical thought. In his Glasgow lectures on moral philosophy, Francis Hutcheson presented "the most complete view of legal philosophy of the time."[15] And those early public lectures Adam Smith delivered in Edinburgh after his return from Oxford (1748–51) in which he first enunciated the principle of the division of labor had as their actual subject matter "jurisprudence," or the philosophy of law.[16] A considerable part of the intellectual history of Scotland in the eighteenth century might be written in terms of direct and indirect legal influences. There was no doubt about the fact that, as one traveler commented late in the century, it was the lawyers who "indeed, in some measure give the tone to the manners of the Scotch Metropolis," that they, "in short, are the principal people in that city."[17]

The similarity in social origins between the Scottish and American literati became evident at a time when another, more complicated relationship between the two societies was being formed. Trade, migration, and cultural exchanges mark one phase of this relationship. But these direct transfers of goods, persons, books, and ideas reflect the profound fact that Scotland and America were provinces, cultural as well as political and economic, of the English-speaking world whose center was London. From this common orientation flowed essential elements of cultural growth.

English sovereignty over the American colonies meant not only regulations and fees, but also the presence of a particular group of men who dominated the stage of colonial affairs. They had first appeared in large numbers in the seventies of the previous century, when, after the settlement of the Restoration government, England had attempted to lace together the scattered segments of its Atlantic empire. To accomplish this, she had dispatched to the centers of settlement royal officials—governors, admirals, customs officials, inspectors of forests, collectors, minor functionaries of all sorts—empowered to assert the prerogatives of sovereignty. In the course of a half-century, the more highly placed of these men, together representing officialdom, became focuses of society in the port towns. Their influence was immense. Not only did they represent political power and economic advantage, but in most urban centers they were models of fashion. More than links between governments, they brought England with them into the heart of colonial America. As the brightest social luminaries in the provincial capitals, they both repelled and attracted. Social groups as well as political factions formed around them.

Officialdom, usually considered a political influence, was in fact a most important shaping force on the formation of colonial society. These agents of imperialism could not help but influence the growth of the arts in the colonies. Arbiters of taste, they attracted, patronized, helped to justify those who devoted themselves to letters, arts, and the graces of life.

In Scotland, too, the political connection with England led public men to become cultural go-betweens. Here, though, it was not an enforced officialdom that mattered; only the hated excisemen correspond in position, and Boswell was unusual in wanting more official Englishmen in Scotland to make the Union more complete. The situation, in fact, was reversed; but the effects were similar. The sixteen peers and forty-five members of Parliament who represented Scotland at Westminster (and who had such a hard time making ends meet in London) brought back English books and English fashions. They were catalysts in the process that gave Edinburgh its own *Tatler,* as well as its coffeehouses and wits, and, later in the century, its gambling clubs and masquerades.

Officialdom in the colonies, Scottish Members of Parliament, the Union of 1707—political relationships between England and her dependencies thus brought about cultural links as well. The existence of imperial agents and local representatives to the cosmopolitan center served also to emphasize the provincial character of life in both regions. Scotsmen and Americans alike were constantly aware that they lived on the periphery of a greater world. The image they held of this world and of their place in it was perhaps the most important, though the subtlest, element common to the cultural growth of America and Scotland in the eighteenth century.

Life in both regions was similarly affected by the mere fact of physical removal from the cosmopolitan center. For though the Scottish border lay less than three hundred miles from London, as late as 1763 only one regular stagecoach traveled between Edinburgh and the British capital. The trip took about two weeks, or fully half the traveling time of the express packet from New York to Falmouth, and those few who could afford to make it considered it so serious an expedition that they frequently made their wills before setting out. As far as the English were concerned, Smollett's Mrs. Tabitha, who thought one could get to Scotland only by sea, represented no great advance over those of her countrymen earlier in the century to whom "many parts of Africa and the Indies . . . are better known than a Region which is contiguous to our own, and which we have always had so great a concern for."[18] Even toward the middle of the century, there were occasions when the London mailbag for Edinburgh was found to contain only a single letter.

But isolation, as Perry Miller has pointed out, "is not a matter of distance or the slowness of communication: it is a question of what a dispatch from distant quarters means to the recipient."[19] News, literature, and personal messages from London did not merely convey information; they carried with them standards by which men and events were judged. In them, as in the personal envoys from the greater European world, was involved a definition of sophistication. *Tatlers* and *Spectators* were eagerly devoured in Edinburgh as in Philadelphia. Scottish ladies, like their American counterparts, ordered all sorts of finery, from dresses to wallpaper, from England. There were Americans who echoed the Scottish minister's complaint that "all the villainous, profane, and obscene books and plays, as printed in London, are got down by Allan Ramsay, and lent out, for an easy price, to young boys, servant weemen of the better sort, and gentlemen."[20] Benjamin Franklin's excitement at first reading the *Spectator* and his grim determination to fashion his own literary style on it is only the most famous example of the passion with which Americans strove to imitate English ways. "I am almost inclined to believe," wrote William Eddis, "that a new fashion is adopted earlier by the polished and affluent Americans, than by many opulent persons in the great metropolis."[21]

Communications from England exerted such authority because they fell upon minds conscious of limited awareness. A sense of inferiority pervaded the culture of the two regions, affecting the great no less than the common. It lay behind David Hume's lament (in 1756) that "we people in the country (for such you Londoners esteem our city) are apt to be troublesome to you people in town; we are vastly glad to receive letters which convey intelligence to us of things we should otherwise have been ignorant of, and can pay them back with nothing but provincial stories which are in no way interesting." And it led Adam Smith to admit that "this country is so barren of all sorts of transactions that can interest anybody that lives at a distance from it that little intertainment is to be expected from any correspondent on this side of the Tweed."[22] It rankled deeply in those like the seventeenth-century cosmopolite John Winthrop Jr., who longingly recalled in "such a wilde place" as Hartford, Connecticut, the excitement of life in the European centers. The young Copley felt it profoundly when he wrote from Boston to Benjamin West in London, "I think myself peculiarly unlucky in Liveing in a place into which there has not been one portrait brought that is worthy to be call'd a Picture within my memory, which leaves me at a great loss to gess the stil that You, Mr. Renolds, and the other Artists pracktice."[23] The young Scot returning to Edinburgh after a journey to the Continent and London felt he had to "labour to tone myself down like an overstrained instrument to the low pitch of the rest about me."[24]

The manners and idioms that labeled the provincial in England were stigmas that Scotsmen and Americans tried to avoid when they could not turn them, like Franklin in Paris, into the accents of nature's own philosopher. There was no subject about which Scotsmen were more sensitive than their speech. Lieutenant Lismahago may have proved to his own satisfaction that "what we generally called the Scottish dialect was, in fact, true, genuine old English," but Dr. Johnson laughed at Hamilton of Bangour's rhyming "wishes" and "bushes," and when, in 1761, Thomas Sheridan, the playwright's father, lectured in Edinburgh (and in Irish brogue) on the art of rhetoric, he had an attentive audience of three hundred nobles, judges, divines, advocates, and men of fashion. Hume kept constantly by his side a list of Scots idioms to be avoided, and was said by Monboddo to have confessed on his deathbed not his sins but his Scotticisms.

By 1754, the emergence of American English, adversely commented on as early as 1735, was so far advanced that the suggestion was made, facetiously, that a glossary of American terms be compiled. The scorn shown by Englishmen for Scots dialect was not heaped upon American speech until after the Revolution. But well before Lexington, Scottish and American peculiarities in language were grouped together as provincial in the English mind, a fact understood by John Witherspoon when he wrote in 1781, "The word Americanism, which I have coined . . . is exactly similar in its formation and signification to the word Scotticism." The same equation of verbal provincialisms underlay Boswell's recounting of an anecdote told him "with great good humour" by the Scottish Earl of Marchmont:

> [T]he master of a shop in London, where he was not known, said to him, "I suppose, Sir, you are an American." "Why so, Sir?" (said his Lordship.) "Because, Sir (replied the shopkeeper,) you speak neither English nor Scotch, but something different from both, which I conclude is the language of America."[25]

The sense of inferiority that expressed itself in imitation of English ways and a sense of guilt regarding local mannerisms was, however, only one aspect of the complex meaning of provincialism. Many Scotsmen and Americans followed the Reverend John Oxenbridge in castigating those who sought to "fashion your selves to the flaunting mode of *England* in worship or walking."[26] In the manner of Ramsay of Ochtertyre's strictures on eighteenth-century Scottish authors, they inveighed against the slavish imitation of English models, such "a confession of inferiority as one would hardly have expected from a proud manly people, long famous for common-sense and veneration for the ancient classics."[27] Awareness of regional limitations frequently led to a compensatory local pride, evolving into a patriotism which was politically effective in the one area and, after the rebellion of 1745, mainly sentimental in the other, due to the diametrically opposed political history of the two—America moving from subordination to independence, Scotland from independence to subordination. It was the conviction that life in the provinces was not merely worthy of toleration by cosmopolites but unique in natural blessings that led Jefferson, in his *Notes on Virginia,* to read the Count de Buffon a lesson in natural history. It was a kindred conviction that, in spite of its "familiarity," life in Edinburgh had a congeniality and vigor all its own, that made Robertson refuse all invitations to settle in London. Hume, too, in the midst of his Parisian triumphs, longed for the "plain roughness" of the Poker Club and the sharpness of Dr. Jardine to correct and qualify the "lusciousness" of French society.[28] Hume's complex attitude toward his homeland is significant; it is typical of a psychology which rarely failed to combat prejudice with pride.

For Scotsmen, this pride was reinforced by the treatment they received in England, where their very considerable successes remained in inverse proportion to their popularity. One day, Ossian, Burns, and Highland tours might help to wipe out even memories of Bute. Meanwhile, in spite of their own "Breetish" Coffee House, life in London was not always easy for visitors from north of the Tweed. "Get home to your crowdie, and be d—d to you! Ha'ye got your parritch yet? When will you get a sheeps-head or a haggis, you ill-far'd lown? Did you ever see meat in Scotland, saving oatmeal hasty pudding? Keep out of his way, Thomas, or you'll get the itch!"[29] The young Scotsman thus recounting his London reception added that there was little real malice behind such common jibes. But Boswell's blood boiled with indignation when he heard shouts of "No Scots, No Scots! Out with them!" at Covent Garden. Yet only a few months later, he may be found addressing a memorandum to himself to "be *retenu* to avoid Scotch sarcasting jocularity," and describing a fellow countryman as "a hearty, honest fellow, knowing and active, but Scotch to the very backbone."[30]

The deepest result of this complicated involvement in British society was that the provincial's view of the world was discontinuous. Two forces, two magnets, affected his efforts to find adequate standards and styles: the values associated with the simplicity and purity (real or imagined) of nativism, and those to be found in cosmopolitan sophistication. Those who could take entire satisfaction in either could maintain a consistent position. But for provincials, exposed to both, an exclusive, singular conception of either kind was too narrow. It meant a rootlessness, an alienation either from the higher sources of culture or from the familiar local environment that had formed the personality. Few whose perceptions surpassed local boundaries rested content with a simple, consistent image of themselves or of the world. Provincial culture, in eighteenth-century Scotland as in colonial America, was formed in the mingling of these visions.

The effect of this situation on cultural growth in the two regions cannot, of course, be measured. Undoubtedly, provincialism sometimes served to inhibit creative effort. But we suggest that there existed important factors which more than balanced the deleterious effects. The complexity of the provincial's image of the world and of himself made demands upon him unlike those felt by the equivalent Englishman. It tended to shake the mind from the roots of habit and tradition. It led men to the interstices of common thought where were found new views and new approaches to the old. It cannot account for the existence of men of genius, but to take it into consideration may help us understand the conditions which fostered in such men the originality and creative imagination that we associate with the highest achievements of the enlightenment in Scotland and America.

8

Peopling the Peripheries

To say anything useful on the occasion of Australia's bicentennial celebration would be difficult enough for anyone not an authority on that nation's history. It becomes far more difficult in view of the publication, in 1987, of the eleven-volume *Australians: A Historical Library*. This massive collaborative work of scholarship conveys not only the complexity of Australia's history but also the learning and imagination of Australia's historians, anthropologists, archaeologists, geographers, and demographers who have shared in this enterprise.

What I might most usefully do relates to the study I have been engaged on for some time, on the peopling of British North America. Nothing in what I have so far done was designed as an exercise in comparative history—none of it was written with an eye on Australian history. But even a cursory survey reveals parallels and significant contrasts between the two histories; and they are at least suggestive of the relationships among all of the settlement colonies in the early British empire.

The scope is immense. One must consider race

relations in Jamaica as well as in New South Wales and the Canadian northwest; settlement policies in Queensland and trans-Appalachia; the Germans in Georgia, in Victoria, and in Nova Scotia; the Scots in Ulster, Queensland, North Carolina, and Prince Edward Island; the fur traders along the Mackenzie, Ohio, Chattahoochie, and Alabama rivers and in the Great Lakes basin; convicts in Maryland, Virginia, and New South Wales; Africans, slaves and free, in the Caribbean islands and in the American South; miscegenation, or the lack of it, in British Columbia, Upper Canada, West Florida, and the Outback. One can only touch the margins of this semiglobal subject and hope to feel one's way toward an understanding of significant relationships.

There are mysteries in all of this, but the starting point at least is clear. The magnitudes of the peopling, or repeopling, process in the borderlands of the early British empire exceed anything of the kind that had occurred before in Western history. The transfer of peoples across vast territories to populate Britain's peripheries—in Ireland, North America, the Caribbean, and the Antipodes—dwarfs anything attempted by the Roman empire, imperial Spain, the Habsburgs, or the *roi-soleil* at the peak of royal French power.

What are the dimensions of the population movements into the first British empire? The figures can only be approximate. From England, in the first century of settlement in the Western Hemisphere, came nearly 400,000 emigrants (a figure equivalent to 69 percent of the entire natural increase of the English population), and in the eighteenth century another 300,000. In addition, some 200,000 Irish (that is, Scotch-Irish Protestants) joined the trans-Atlantic migration before 1776, as did close to 100,000 German-speaking people and, involuntarily, no less than 1,744,000 Africans of mixed ethnicities drawn principally from the hinterlands of the Gulf of Guinea, the vast region at the eastward bend of the African coast, now the sites of the Ivory Coast, Ghana, Nigeria, and Cameroon. The estimated total number of people, therefore, transferred to British territory in the Western Hemisphere before 1776 is approximately 2,744,000 souls, in a period in which the total population of Britain itself rose to only eight and a half million.

The contrast with the other imperial powers in the West is striking. From France (population approximately twenty million) to New France came a total of less than 30,000 people in the entire colonial period, though an estimated 636,000 African slaves were exported to the French Caribbean islands. And while Spain's trans-Atlantic emigration was much larger than that of the French, the ratio of Spain's emigrants to its domestic population was less than half that of Britain's. At the end of the first century of their respective colonization efforts, the number of Britons or their descendants in British America was twice that of the peninsular Spaniards and Creoles in Spanish America. In each of the two short peak periods of population movements from Britain to America, 1630–60 and 1760–76, the flow totaled close to a quarter of a million people.

These are key facts somehow obscured by historians of the empire concentrating on institutions, power rivalries, cultural transfers, and trade. They lie at the heart of the social history of the eighteenth-century empire. Everything flows from them. Without a general knowledge of how this movement of people came about and what forces or desires impelled or drew these people from one continent to another, little can be understood of the history of any area of settlement: North America, the Caribbean, or, I believe, Australia.

What accounts for this movement of people? Several forces seem to be obvious. The first is simply greed—or more politely, entrepreneurial zeal—the passion for profits and the ruthless, buccaneering spirit of the British entrepreneurs of the seventeenth and eighteenth centuries. The merchants and their coinvestors among the gentry are everywhere in the history of the first empire, and everywhere they account for some significant part of the peopling—or repeopling—of the colonial territories. The investors in the Virginia Company (1607–24) put up approximately £100,000—something like £10 million in modern money—in their failing effort to extract precious metals from the colony's soil, or reduce the native population to a useful labor force, or find the fabled passage through to the Pacific. But while six out of seven of the more than 8,500 servants and free settlers they sent over died before the company was dissolved, 1,275 survived. These survivors, dirt-grubbing but ambitious tobacco farmers who operated in the tight grip of British tobacco merchants, were soon importing annually some 1,500 indentured servants shipped mainly via London and Bristol, who formed the demographic basis of what became one of Britain's premier colonies. And the Virginia colony was typical. In all, eleven commercial companies poured approximately £13 million into North American and Caribbean settlement efforts before 1640, and while few of their original plans prospered, in the process they sent thousands of English men, women, and children to create communities from Maine to the coast of Nicaragua.

These were Creole communities, their population drawn from abroad. For those of the indigenous peoples who had survived devastating foreign diseases, race wars, and disorienting changes in their once familiar environments had proved useless to the British as a labor force and constituted a declining part of the population. Unlike the Spanish and the French, the British did not easily merge with native peoples—in Alabama or in Connecticut or in Limerick, Jamaica, or Queensland. In Spanish America, by the end of the colonial period, an estimated 40 percent of the population was *mestizo*. In Britain's colonies, officially recognized miscegenation was almost nonexistent. Interracial sex relations could, of course, be found everywhere, and there were mixed-blood children in every colony. But these relations were almost always clandestine—at worst the product of rape, at best concubinage—and they did not produce a significant portion of the population.[1] In only one area of the British peripheries in this era were such relations official and demographically and culturally important—in the fur-trading society of western Canada, where a unique form of interracial marriage rites developed, marriages, as they said, *à la façon du pays,* which combined aboriginal and British marriage customs.

During the initial stages of the fur trade, when the traders—hundreds of miles out into the far northwest interior—were dependent upon the Indians for survival, formal and stable alliances with Indian women became a central part of the fur traders' world, and a mixed-blood population resulted. The close-knit Anglo-Indian families made the traders' lives bearable; but it was a transitory phase. Mixed-blood girls, the products of these marriages, were led away from their Indian heritage (as their brothers were not), encouraged to imitate the ways of European women, and merge with the European population. And when European women appeared in the Canadian West, first in the Earl of Selkirk's Red River settlement of 1812, the mixed-race women found themselves disoriented: marginalized and the victims of overpowering racist sentiment.[2]

But all of this is unique. Intimate relations between the English and the native Irish—people the English considered as barbarous and primitive as the American aborigines—were few before the nineteenth century (in the fourteenth century such unions had been altogether banned), perhaps no more numerous than Anglo-Algonquin or Anglo-Iroquoian relations. When, as with Sir William Johnson at his biracial establishment along the Mohawk River in the 1760s, stable relations between respectable British men and native women occurred openly and officially, it was considered a remarkable development. Lord Adam Gordon, visiting Johnson's baronial court, cleared, he reported, "in an absolute forest," was astonished and repelled by what he saw. "No consideration," he wrote, "should tempt me to lead [Sir William's] life. . . . I know no other man equal to so disagreeable a duty."[3]

But if the natives and their progeny were not able to supply the necessary labor, other sources would be found—first, indentured servants from the homeland, bound to four or five years of service. Between one-half and two-thirds of all those brought to the Western Hemisphere by the British in the seventeenth and eighteenth centuries were brought over in some such condition of bonded servitude. When the expanding plantation economy demanded more labor than could be supplied by white servants, Africans were imported as slaves: that is, as *chattel* slaves.

Chattel slavery, the most debased form of bondage, was not something inherited from the past or borrowed from the Mediterranean or South America. Slavery elsewhere and at other times had mollifying elements, elements that softened the rigor of absolute debasement. Chattel slavery had none. In its most extreme form it evolved in British America, took form in British-American law in response to the need for a totally reliable, totally exploitable, and infinitely recruitable labor force.

• • •

Wherever the possibility of profits existed—and it existed almost everywhere in these raw borderlands—merchant adventurers appeared to exploit it. And almost everywhere their efforts involved not mergers with native peoples but the recruitment of people from elsewhere—settlers to make rentable or salable farms out of wild land, laborers to dig the mines, man the iron works, build the houses, bridges, roads, and ships, and slaves to work in the plantations.

Syndicates were formed to exploit the recruitment of Protestant Germans—syndicates that included general managers in Britain; recruiting agents at key rendezvous spots in the Rhineland; hawkers and promoters in the villages and farmlands; Dutch, German, and English shippers; merchants in the Western Hemisphere to sell, at ports of entry, the services of those who could not pay for their passage.

The marketing of British servants and African slaves flowed through structures of trans-Atlantic commerce; it responded, though not always sensitively, to fluctuations in colonial labor needs and came in time to embrace an astonishing range in space. Servants recruited in the depths of London's slums or in hiring fairs in the remote English countryside were hawked through the backcountry of the Chesapeake colonies, a hundred miles from the Atlantic coast, peddled at the docks of the West Indian ports, and bought by speculators like Washington to open farms in the wilderness of Ohio. And English slave traders, in intricate transaction cycles, linked Liverpool and a few other English ports to villages deep in the West African hinterland and to plantations scattered on Caribbean islands and the American Deep South.

Australia was founded in a period, opened by the British victories of the Seven Years' War, that saw the most concentrated burst of entrepreneurial energies directed overseas since the age of James I. At the crack of the conquest of Canada, with the smell of gunpowder still high on the Plains of Abraham, Scottish merchants, assisted by New Englanders, lunged on the entrepôt of Montreal, absorbed the resources and personnel of the defeated French, and in a short period of time built an elaborate network of inland trade. At the time Arthur Phillip and his fleet entered Sydney Harbour, the St. Lawrence traders, after saturating the *Petit Nord* (between Lake Winnipeg and Hudson's Bay), were reaching far beyond the range of the earlier French traders, to the great divide between Hudson's Bay and the Arctic drainages, twenty-five hundred miles northwest of Montreal. In this remote, uncharted region, frozen for much of the year, the North West Company and its predecessor and competitor, the Hudson's Bay Company, sent a veritable regiment of traders, trappers, and guides. During the first decade and a half of New South Wales's life as a British colony, when the British population in Australia rose to seven thousand, these two Canadian companies alone maintained around two thousand permanent employees. Many were French Canadians, but among them too were Scots, English, and Irish. Three quarters of the Hudson's Bay Company's employees in the northwest posts were brought over from the Orkney Islands. In these northern forests the Indian population fell to a ratio of one to six with the Europeans.

In the same interwar years, far to the south, the same frantic exploitation took place in the humid jungles and hot scrub fields of East and West Florida, acquired from Spain in the same treaty that gave Britain Canada.

That remarkable passage of British overseas history, almost exactly contemporaneous with the settlement of Australia, reads like a dark, Faulknerian novel. Conceived of—like seventeenth-century Virginia, Barbados, Providence Island, and Bermuda—as a bonanza world in which immense fortunes could be made by those adventurous and energetic enough to survive the inevitable rigors, the Floridas proved to be a tropical graveyard for thousands of settlers, bond and free.

One high-flying westcountryman sank £20,000 in an attempt to establish a profitable plantation amid the inland swamps and pine barrens of northeast Florida, bringing over a crowd of vagrants, beggars, and debtors he collected out of the London jails. They may have been, as they were described at the time, a troop of "shoe blacks, cheminy sweepers . . . cinder wenches, whores and pickpockets,"[4] but they were not chained convicts, and they were not fools. They took one look at the hot, swampy jungle and the tangles of palmettos they were told to tear out by the roots, ignored their indentures, and fled.

All sorts of efforts were made to populate the Floridas—with anyone: Huguenots, Bermudians, Irish, Germans, Swiss, Scottish Highlanders, even some of the prostitutes being rehabilitated in London's Magdalen House. Sir Alexander Grant, who dreamed up the idea of transporting the prostitutes to Florida, confessed, with not exactly stunning insight, "Tis true they are not virgins"; nevertheless, he said, they would surely make splendid wives and mothers for such as were likely to live in a place like Florida.[5] And in the most bizarre case of all, three influential Londoners, including the former prime minister George Grenville, collected some fourteen hundred Greeks, Corsicans, Italians, and Minorcans to settle a plantation inside the well-named Mosquito Inlet, seventy-five miles south of St. Augustine. There, in the pestilential, snake-filled swamps, these indentees, who had hoped to escape persecution and poverty in their homelands, died in droves. Even a reign of terror imposed by brutal overseers could not turn them into a useful labor force. Some survived and fled north when the American Revolution threw everything into confusion. Only slaves could be forced to do the necessary work, and so it was that gradually, on the more salubrious coastal islands, on a few inland farms, at spots along the coast of the Gulf of Mexico and in the rich Mississippi Delta, a sprawling, almost completely ungoverned plantation society emerged freely—a society of British or Anglo-American masters and a workforce of slaves brought in from the West Indies, the East Coast slave markets, or Africa.

Thus the merchants, the City men and their gentry allies with money to invest, dreaming of extracting fortunes from the exploitation of the colonial world, became involved in financing, managing, and sustaining the movement of people from the major population centers of Europe or from Africa to the labor-short marchlands of the western colonies.

But the movement of people in such large numbers is not accounted for only by such entrepreneurial zeal. A powerful, self-intensifying impetus was created when these far borderlands came to be seen not only as a target for exploitation and a labor market but as a world where a measure of independence and security could be found by individual farmers, farm-workers, and artisans denied those advantages at home and willing to risk everything to obtain them.

The voluntary movements of such husbandmen and artisans seeking not simply employment but new, more secure and hopeful lives on the land in the peripheries began with the first wave of Scots into northern Ireland in the early seventeenth century and simultaneously of English settlers into the still-undefined economies of the West Indies. The flow intensified steadily through the Williamite settle-ments in Ireland and the opening, first, of the Caro-linas, then of the Delaware colonies (New Jersey and Pennsylvania), then of upcountry New York and New England, and finally, after 1760, of Nova Scotia, Prince Edward Island, and what is now the province of New Brunswick. To these territories land-seeking family groups, especially from northern Britain, be-gan a movement which would end in a flood. Just as tens of thousands of Scots sought independence and relief from poverty by crossing the Irish Sea and becoming tenants on lands seized from the Irish in the three great waves of English confiscations in Ireland, so other thousands moved off to establish homesteads in the Maritime Provinces, New York and Vermont, the backcountry of the Upper South, and isolated enclaves like the future Fayetteville, North Carolina, which by 1760 was as Scottish as Aberdeen.

It is true that many, if not most, of the multitude of indentured servants who peopled the peripheral lands were completely impoverished and had little choice but to follow the dictates of those who would finance their transportation. But others of some small substance adopted indentured servitude as an economic strategy. Holding in reserve a fund for the future, they wrote off the work itself as a valuable introduction to the ways of a new world.

These were migrants with genteel aspirations, dreams of respectable and independent establishments. They were voluntary migrants seeking security, freedom from poverty and chronic underemployment, and an independent stake in the land—attractions that were as powerful in the seventeenth and eighteenth centuries as they would be in the nineteenth century when, for the same reasons, thousands of emigrants left the British Isles for Australia. Their sacrifices to gain the security they sought were sometimes heroic, often tragic.

Those who migrated as indentured servants left very few records in which one can glimpse their inner lives, but the uprooting and migration of the husbandmen and farmworkers from Yorkshire and the clansmen from the Highlands and the Scottish islands are well documented. The diaries, letters, public reports, and newspaper accounts reveal scenes of wrenching departures, terrifying and sometimes fatal experiences at sea, and ultimately the disorientation of resettlement in a strange new world. The lands on which they settled seemed vacant; at best they were thinly peopled with aborigines with whom the settlers would not assimilate. It was a world that lacked for these Europeans the dense social texture that had always enclosed them. Life on an isolated farm on Prince Edward Island or in the Genesee or Shenandoah valleys, or near Augusta, Pensacola, or Natchez was profoundly different from life on a tenancy in County Down or Dorset. There was no human context. Nothing was prescribed, ascribed, given. Removed from the subtly modulated society they had known, the settlers would be bereft and reduced. Independence was enriching, but most often it meant loss, isolation, and cultural deprivation, and while in time their children, if not they themselves, would build structured societies from these isolated settlements, they would not reproduce the texture of European life.

In this the parallels are striking. Migrants on farms along Australia's Murray, Darling, and Macquarie rivers experienced the same isolation and deprivation as settlers on the Mohawk, the Savannah, and the Mississippi, who came from the same British world; they developed the same sense of independence; the ordering of their lives was equally fragile; violence was similarly common; and they suffered similar kinds of despair. Patrick White's *The Tree of Man* is a great novel, hence both unique and universal. But its elegiac portrayal of isolated suffering and of the evanescence of human achievement is something, I believe, shared by all the peripheral worlds. It is closer to Faulkner than to Galsworthy, to Melville than to Dickens.

The costs were great, but whatever the cost, hundreds of thousands of people willingly moved out to these marginal worlds. However unknown and mysterious they were, these were seen as lands of opportunity—even the most thickly populated plantation region of the long-settled West Indies, which had ceased attracting homesteaders. It is revealing that the register of British emigrants compiled in the years just before the American Revolution—a unique document of the premodern years—shows peculiar variations for those emigrating to the Caribbean. They were predominantly young, single men, but unlike single men headed elsewhere in the Western Hemisphere, very few of them were indentured servants. They were free men, of some little substance, and their stated occupations were unique. While in the British emigration as a whole only 2 percent were registered as "gentlemen," the percentage of "gentlemen" among the prospective West Indians was 22 percent; and while only 5 percent of the migrants as a whole said their work involved merchandising, 30 percent of those traveling to the islands said that. And their reasons for emigrating were overwhelmingly and uniquely positive: 94 percent of those embarking for the West Indies said they expected to settle as planters or estate owners, buy land or other property, or follow their previous occupations; only 21 percent in the migration as a whole were as confident of the future.

There is no mystery in any of this. While the West Indian plantations had no place for free white laborers, unskilled artisans, or married homesteaders, they did have a place for well-connected, single young men with capital to invest, or young men experienced in trade, bookkeeping, and management, or highly skilled craftsmen whose skills could not be supplied by well-trained plantation slaves. No doubt many of these migrants to the islands expected to return home, though how many actually did we will never know. They were, however, part of a vast flow of people who saw a better, more hopeful, and more secure world overseas and took advantage of whatever means they could find to relocate themselves there. They were not victims shunted unwillingly from place to place, but adventurous risk-takers willing to gamble everything they had known for the prospect that glowed from abroad.

The migration to the underdeveloped borderlands

proved to be self-intensifying. The new settlements everywhere led to the appreciation of land values, which in turn stimulated fevers of land speculation, and speculators—some British, some colonial—became active agents of population recruitment. Land claims that had been ignored because they were valueless in the seventeenth century were resecured in the eighteenth century as population grew and their potential value became obvious. So the Earl Granville inherited, and through his agents helped populate, the northern half of North Carolina; so Lord Fairfax inherited and profitably populated the five million acres of the Northern Neck of Virginia, which had been granted to his family in 1649; so the Penn and Calvert families inherited from seventeenth-century grants title to the undistributed lands of Pennsylvania and Maryland.

But these were only the most spectacular of a veritable battalion of land speculators who, in large ways and small, helped propel the migrations forward. Large networks developed, involving principals with claims to uncultivated land, working through agents in Britain, Ireland, and the German states who conducted elaborate recruiting campaigns in areas of social discontent or rapid economic change.

One can occasionally trace the elaborate filiations of those recruiting networks—for example, from the Duke of Rutland's modernizing properties in Yorkshire, through operators working out of Hull, Liverpool, or Whitehaven, to land speculators at the head of the Bay of Fundy in Nova Scotia; or from obscure villages in the Palatinate and the Upper Rhineland and Switzerland, through intricate passages along the tributaries of the Rhine and through that river itself to Rotterdam, thence to Cowes, Philadelphia, and ultimately to farms along the Susquehanna and the Mohawk rivers. Land speculation fed on the desire for security and independence, and in turn stimulated the aspirations upon which it fed.

But beyond these forces at work propelling and drawing people outward from their original locations to very different worlds on Britain's far-distant peripheries, there was another propellant, less commonly understood at the time, perhaps less visible and deliberate, but powerful nevertheless. It is a force that links Australia to the other peripheries, especially to North America, most directly.

The purpose of government in the seventeenth and eighteenth centuries was simply to govern, that is, to keep order under law and maintain security and stability in domestic and foreign affairs. The solution of social problems was not Parliament's chief mandate, and it rarely acted as if it were. Despite a few famous enactments like the Statute of Artificers (1563) or two centuries later the Gin Act (1751), there was no tradition of such social regulation by this mercantilist state. What we now call the administrative infrastructure for such matters did not exist at the national level, nor was the organization of society sufficiently threatened, except by the rising numbers of poor, to warrant a more active, interventionist state. Yet social problems certainly existed; and they were in part relieved by the absorptive capacity of the colonies.

England's urban populations were volatile; mobs formed easily, and once inflamed were difficult to control. Again and again the discontented, the impoverished, and the politically fearful turned to public agitation, which grew more dangerous with the increase in the number of participants. The government-sanctioned emigration of some 400,000 working people in the course of a century during which the combined populations of London and Bristol grew from 215,000 to only 600,000 must have had a decisive effect in easing social strains. And that moderating effect must have continued as wave after wave of brief but severe depressions hit the lurching urban economies and thousands of emigrants left Britain's shores annually with the government's tacit approval.

Throughout this entire era the colonies were Britain's safety valves, just as later the American West would be seen as a safety valve for the relatively deprived of the eastern states. All sorts of social and political problems were involved.

As early as the 1570s plans were made to transport Lancashire Catholics to Ireland to serve the queen in that borderland in exchange for toleration; and shortly thereafter a plan was floated to settle three thousand Puritans on that same frontier. Nothing came of those schemes, but in 1597 a more realistic plan was devised to settle the dissenting separatists, the Brownists, some of whom would later become famous as the American Pilgrims, on the Magdalen Islands in the Gulf of St. Lawrence. Lord Burghley himself was interested, and the queen licensed the Pilgrims to settle there, to fish and to hunt walruses and whales—so long as they agreed to stay there, safely out of England, until they were willing to conform in religion. An advance party made it safely to the Magdalens but was fought off by hostile Basque and French fishermen, and the project was abandoned.

By then the precedent was established. In the seventeenth century the government similarly acquiesced in the Pilgrims' plan to emigrate to Virginia (their settling in Plymouth was not planned) and then to charter the Puritans' exodus to Massachusetts. Later, the crown was even more active in chartering Penn's extensive colony in America, in part to relieve the country of the equally obnoxious Quakers.

But religious dissent was a problem of decreasing importance in the eighteenth century. Its place was taken by poverty and crime, and again the government turned to the colonies for relief. The chartering of the colony of Georgia in 1732 was an official endorsement of the strenuous efforts that philanthropists like James Oglethorpe and the Earl of Egmont were making to solve, or at least relieve, the growing problem of poverty. The Georgia colony's twenty-one trustees were close students of Britain's social problems; ten of them had been members of the Commons' committee on the state of the jails (1729), and most of them were involved in efforts to relieve imprisoned debtors. By shipping the deserving poor—that is, exporting the problem—to the southern borderland of Britain's mainland territories, they and the government hoped to ease the social problem for which they had no domestic solution, and at the same time to build a barrier against Spanish and French expansion in the South and improve Britain's trade balance by increasing the production of colonial goods. It was a mixture of motives that would be repeated fifty-six years later in the settlement of Australia.

The Georgia scheme was clever and elaborate—too clever. It suffered from, indeed was destroyed by, an excess of logic. Alcohol was banned by the Georgia trustees, and so too were black slaves—because, logically, both would corrupt the diligence that the trustees hoped to develop in their charges. Private property was limited, to preclude the corruption of wealth, and the settlers were carefully screened for virtue and

industry sufficient to guarantee the moral development of the community. The aim, above all, was to
transform the national burden of a growing body of
indigents, draining the substance of the land and con-
tributing nothing, into the advantage of a productive
colonial labor force whose moral character would be
improved by hard work in a healthy environment.

Though the colony of Georgia eventually succeeded, Oglethorpe's project failed. The trustees' principles were quickly overthrown: alcohol, slaves, and
unlimited landholdings all soon appeared, and the
elaborate screening process by which the worthy poor
were to be sifted out from the mass of the merely des-
titute broke down. Modern historians estimate that
perhaps one-third of the entire British population
lived at or under the poverty line, but the trustees,
in their twenty years of corporate existence, were
able to certify and transport to Georgia only a total
of 2,122 charity cases, and that with public subsidies
of £155,700 (almost twice as much as the cost of Australia's First Fleet). As the trustees' control lapsed,
the general peopling of the colony, by employees
of ambitious entrepreneurs and by self-supporting
homesteaders, developed in a rush.

Still, the trustees' aims were by no means repudi-
ated. Their scheme proved to be a model for others.
The Board of Trade considered seriously similar plans
for the subsidized transportation of the English poor

to Maine, Jamaica, the Bahamas, the Virgin Islands, North and South Carolina, and Nova Scotia—plans that were not basically different from the later assisted immigration schemes which in the nineteenth century would bring three-quarters of a million immigrants to Australia.

In small matters and large, again and again, the government turned to managing the movement of people out to the western peripheries. To develop needed naval stores during the War of Spanish Succession it sent over to the Mohawk valley in upcountry New York three thousand Protestant Germans, part of a larger contingent whose migration to England the government had subsidized, some of whom were eventually sent off to Ireland. To secure its possession of Nova Scotia in 1748, after the fortress of Louisbourg on Cape Breton had been returned to the French, the British government again turned to subsidized migration. It sent off, at great expense, to the naval base and provincial capital newly established at Halifax a first fleet—so called, in Halifax's history—of over twenty-five hundred disbanded soldiers and sailors, London artisans, and migrant Irish. They followed that shipment with twenty-seven hundred more settlers drawn from the German states, the Netherlands, Switzerland, and Lorraine.

Solving as it did such a range of public problems by the transfer of people to the outer reaches of its jurisdiction, the British government naturally conceived of eliminating or relieving its growing prison population by the same means. The seventeenth-century colonies were thought of not only as crude, quite barbarous places, exile to which was in itself a punishment, but also to some degree as military garrisons, where stricter discipline could be imposed than in the home islands.[6] So, in the seventeenth century, the practice developed of sending convicts, along with prisoners of war, to labor in the colonies, despite growing objections from the settlers that the colonies would be corrupted by such villainous characters and would come to be thought of as "a hell upon earth, another Siberia." After the Transportation Statute of 1718 regularized, indeed mandated, the subsidized transportation of convicted felons to North America, the small irregular trickle of immigrant convicts grew into a steady flow. By 1776 an estimated total of forty thousand had been sent to the North American colonies, almost exactly the same number that were to come to Australia (New South Wales and Tasmania) through 1824, when the system changed. In the relatively small area of Maryland to which they were sent they came to constitute between 10 and 12 percent of the free adult working population.[7]

There is much in this early, North American phase of the transportation system that was similar to what came later in Australia. The criminal laws that sent these thousands to America as an alternative to capital punishment were largely the same as those that convicted Australia's first settlers. The judicial system was the same, and the social background of the convicts and the kinds of crimes they committed were largely the same. Yet there were fundamental differences in terms of results, and this was not simply because Australia is five and a half times farther from Britain than is the East Coast of America.

I might put the difference most simply this way: I have never found a reference to a convict in any genealogy or history of an American family, nor in any other way does a single one of the forty thousand convicts sent to America appear as such. Beyond occasional registration in the initial port of entry (records that were kept erratically) and references in a few of the surviving record books of merchants and plantation owners, and beyond the ads for runaways in the newspapers, there are no records of these convicts. They seem to have faded into the general population, casting no shadows, leaving no tracks. As for their lives in America, far from suffering degradation, savage punishments, or lifelong stigmatization, they seem to have found, even in their bondage, release and a measure of freedom. For, as was remarked again and again, life in bondage in America was for them, if not more easeful, then less threatening, far healthier, and more hopeful than what they had known before.

This was true also, we now know, for many convicts in Australia, but to a lesser degree, and the difference in degree is significant. For almost all of the convicts sent to the west, America proved from the beginning to be a bountiful, not a fatal, shore.

The reasons for this are in part obvious. America was not a penal camp. It was a developing, increasingly genteel but labor-short society, and the punishment imposed on the convicts was, technically, not hard labor but exile for seven or more years. Convicts with a little money, by paying for their passage and other costs, could buy freedom from labor, though not from exile. Of course, since almost all of them were penniless, the great majority immediately became bond servants, and were sold along with the voluntary indentees.

And that was the key to their fates. The central process of the transportation system in pre-Revolutionary America was the integration of the convict population into the general servant population by means of the contractors' desire to profit by the sale of the convicts' labor to private employers. Paid £5 a head by the government to get rid of the convicts, the contractors did everything they could to maximize the price they could sell them for. To overcome the convicts' obvious disadvantages in the open labor market—their physical decrepitude, especially after long confinement, their presumed willfulness and determination to escape, and their familiarity with, if not habituation to, crime and general disorder—the contractors and the retail merchandisers of servants tried to merge the convicts with the free servants; tried to make the convicts lose their identities. It was simply good business. Some merchants hid the convicts' backgrounds, until forced by the colonial governments to reveal them; some avoided whenever possible using the words "convict" and "felon," and stressed as strongly as they could the convicts' skills as artisans, farmhands, or sailors. Most American employers, on the other hand, tried to identify the convicts and to avoid buying them if they could; but in the end, the pull of the labor market, especially in certain districts of Virginia and Maryland, overcame their scruples, and they bought them (as cheaply as possible) along with other servants, trusting to luck that the convicts would prove to be manageable, hardworking, and respectful of the law.

The convict experience in America was altogether different from what it later proved to be in Australia. The convicts in America were not confined to an outdoor prison beyond the possibility of return. In Australian terms, they were all working under the assignment system from the start, subject not to public but to private control, to employers who were dependent on them. Some convicts did experience harsh treatment by brutal masters who beat them and forced them into chains and iron collars when they tried to escape. But this was rare, and there was no possibility of returning them to government service for punishment. More painful to most than physical punishment was the acute loneliness and disorientation they experienced on remote dirt farms deep in the Chesapeake interior, and the humiliation of working long hours side by side with the most degraded white servants, occasionally with slaves.

There were no penal taskmasters, no floggers, no Norfolk Island or other inhumane centers of secondary punishment. There was no government control. The masters who bought the convicts were the only people who counted, and what they wanted was not reformation or punishment for past crimes but work, cheap labor. Harsh treatment was simply counterproductive—especially since the convicts, living without confinement with other servants, could easily escape. An estimated 9 percent, in the most populous areas of convict settlement, did so. Those smart enough could manage to escape home. For by the mid-eighteenth century the Atlantic shipping lanes were crowded with vessels of all kinds, and convicts could easily change identities and get jobs on shipboard, scrape up enough to pay their passage, or stow away. At times this was done in collusion with gang members at home, and so some of the convicts were drawn back into their old haunts, where, under threat of immediate execution for escaping from their exile, they could be blackmailed by London's crime bosses into becoming point men of thieving rings.

So the peopling of the British peripheries proceeded, propelled by business enterprise; by the desires of the discontented, the threatened, and those ambitious for a greater measure of security and independence; by land speculation; and by the efforts of the government and private philanthropists to relieve major social problems by exporting them. The resulting British settlement colonies, especially those in mainland North America and Australia, though they developed in different physical environments and had varied ethnic compositions, had similar characteristics.

Unlike the Spanish, Portuguese, Dutch, and French colonies, where the native populations were brought within the control of governing Creoles and European-born crown officers and were subject, too, to the discipline of the church, the British settlement colonies were repopulated with their own people, with similar Europeans, or in the Western Hemisphere with Africans. These loose societies were spread out thinly through huge territories—Rupert's Land, trans-Appalachia, the tablelands of the Great Dividing Range and the western plains beyond—where one found isolated people, struggling in family or small, scattered community groups, in an environment lightly touched by human cultivation, flung open for exploitation.

Ethnically homogeneous these colonies were not. From almost the earliest years there were English, Irish, Scots, and soon thereafter Germans, Swiss, Dutch, and other north Europeans, followed by a variety of Mediterranean peoples and in America a multitude of Africans of various ethnic backgrounds.

But violent they were—violent beyond the measure of British life. Britain's cities, especially London in its darker pockets, were at times dangerous places. Crime syndicates dominated sections of the city, and violent crime in the countryside was commonplace. But if there were well-organized crime bands in London and highwaymen on the post roads of Britain—if there were footpads, thieves, and thugs of all sorts—there were no bushrangers, as in Australia. Nor were there brutalized war veterans, as in South Carolina, who hid with runaway slaves in inaccessible backcountry forests and swamps, from which they emerged to devastate the countryside, kidnapping and torturing planters and tradesmen who refused to reveal the whereabouts of their valuables. Nor were there so-called Regulators who set out to rid the country of such savages, only to become themselves so brutal that they in turn had to be fought off by other vigilantes who called themselves Moderators. And nowhere in Britain was there bloody race warfare or the brutality of chattel slavery, which bred a callousness in human relations that generations of growing gentility would only gradually—if ever—eradicate.

For gentility, the self-conscious civility of ambitious colonial societies, rose quickly in these remote British colonies, and the dominance of British middle-class culture was established. Just as the small population of Sydney and its suburbs acquired, in an astonishingly short period of time, the appearance of Home County gentility—just as the Cumberland Plain took on the appearance, within two decades of the founding, of a veritable recreation of the peaceful English countryside—so Philadelphia, Boston, New York, and Charleston became familiar provincial British towns with parkland suburbs. And the more affluent plantations in the South—Monticello, Mount Vernon, Sabine Hill—became showplaces of rural sophistication. But savagery lurked at the edges everywhere—in the border regions of the Cumberland Plain near Sydney as in eastern Kentucky; along the Murrumbidgee in New South Wales as well as the Monongahela in Pennsylvania; in the killing fields of Myall Creek and Fallen Timbers; and in the entire plantation world of the Caribbean and the southern mainland colonies. Everyone, however sheltered, knew about the savagery and experienced it at least vicariously.

The more affluent settlers in Australia and in the American colonies may have read the *Spectator* and the *Gentleman's Magazine;* they may have built private libraries, bought and used silver tea services, and cultivated formal gardens. But they knew of, and some participated in, the carnage of the Cherokee War (1760–61), just as they knew of the slaughter of the Indians by the Paxton Boys in Lancaster, Pennsylvania, thirty miles from Philadelphia, a seesawing conflict that Benjamin Franklin—scientist and *philosophe,* the apotheosis of the Enlightenment—was called upon to arbitrate. So too in bustling, bourgeois Sydney, everyone knew of the fierce race conflicts that shot up like rings of fire around the major areas of settlement—first along the Hawkesbury, then along the Hunter, and by the 1830s in the Namoi River valley. But there is no clear geography of these murderous conflicts. Like the massacres at Bolivia Station in the far north of New South Wales and at Fighting Hills in western Victoria, they erupted everywhere along the shifting points of contact between the races, until the natives, in Australia as in America, were destroyed or driven into remote corners of the Outback. Hobart was a civilized town, but guerrilla warfare was the basic fact of life in Tasmania until the entire native population was wiped out in a systematic program of extermination. There was no insulation from this brutality, any more than there was from the knowledge of convict rebellions, which led to bloody reprisals—just as did the many attempted slave revolts that terrified the white populations of mainland North America and the Caribbean islands.

This mixture of growing gentility and persistent brutality, of civility and violence, was common to all of the borderland worlds. But there were subtler similarities too—similarities in the awareness of cultural marginality, of inferiority to the core culture "at home," and acceptance of the homelander's view of the peripheries as, if not primitive, then deeply provincial, hence derivative and inferior.

In all of this the parallels between early British Australia and early British America are particularly striking. But however similar these two sets of settlement colonies may have been, there are major differences too in their historical foundations and development.

First, from the beginning early Australia developed within the control of a central authority. America did not. Alan Frost, in his biography of Arthur Phillip, puts the point forcefully. Phillip's commission and his instructions, Frost writes, gave him

> immediate supervision of the activities of such subordinate officers as the deputy judge—advocate who administered the law; of the commissary, who fed the party; of the surgeon, who kept them healthy; and of the

commandant of marines, who guarded them. It also allowed him to take direct responsibility for town planning, for agriculture, for land-granting, and for policing and penal policies. Phillip's long training as a naval officer and his experience in captaining large warships led him naturally into exercising this authority, which he did insistently. He chose the site, and he planned the town to rise about it. He oversaw the physical operation of the colony in all its details. He directed groups of colonists to other sites, and sent ships out into the world to obtain supplies. He mediated in the bitter quarrels between the officers. He supervised the administration of justice, and he dispensed the King's mercy.[8]

And this central control, though progressively moderated and checked by democratic institutions, continued to guide Australia's development.

There is no parallel to this in seventeenth- or eighteenth-century British America, despite the efforts that were made to create what have been called "garrison governments." The effective governments that existed were highly decentralized, and emerged from within the communities themselves. When in the later eighteenth century Britain attempted to rationalize and coordinate the scattered authorities that had developed, they found themselves faced with popular resistance as hard and complex as a coral reef. The royal governors were helpless in the face of popular opposition. British law in America was pervasive and strong, because locally useful; British authority was a superficial structure lightly imposed on a scattering of largely self-sufficient political communities. Nowhere could Locke's contract theory of government have made more sense. When independent governments were formed during the Revolution, they grew not from a central source out and down into the subordinate branches of government, but from the bottom up, from town and county meetings to county conventions and provincial congresses, finally culminating in a weak representative national congress. And thereafter, in the national period, central authority grew slowly. The effective force of the American national government was weak until the Civil War. Its great regulatory powers, exercised now by all three branches of the national government, are a product largely of the late nineteenth and the twentieth centuries, and are still subject to powerful counter-forces from below.

Second, though both American and Australian settlers believed the indigenous peoples, with exceptions in certain regions and enterprises, were useless as a labor force and drove them from the land, and though both established much of their early economies on the exploitation of imported unfree labor—on the one hand slaves, on the other convicts—there were fundamental differences in the demographic outcomes. The servitude of the convicts was, so to speak, self-liquidating. It existed in most cases for a stated number of years (at most a quarter were sentenced for life); it could not be passed on to a second generation; and it was not associated with race. Portia Robinson's *The Hatch and Brood of Time,* which traces the family life and children of the convicts, could have no parallel in American historiography. For while convicts and indentured servants melded into the general population, the slaves did not. The children of slaves were slaves, and after emancipation succeeding generations carried with them the identity of a distinctive race. Robinson's book demonstrates how the children of the convicts, who "had severed all contact with their convict parents," merged naturally into the mainstream of the nation's life. A century and a half after emancipation much of the black population of North America is still struggling to do the same.[9]

And third, American nationality was forged in an eighteenth-century Enlightenment revolution. The nation's political and ideological identity did not slowly evolve, it exploded. If there had been no Revolution, America, like Australia and Canada, would eventually have become independent. But its independence would have been the product of a gradual attenuation from Britain, developing through a long phase of colonial nationalism, which would have preserved residues of the old status, political and cultural, and hence would have produced a rather different world from what exists today.

For the Revolution built into American political ideology the idealism of the reformers of the eighteenth century, and led to systems of government, national and local, that scatter rather than concentrate the uses of power. And it rejected the basic principles of a hierarchical society. Its powerful ideology transformed what had been seen as the negative, regressive, provincial characteristics of a borderland world into the positive identity of a new, more enlightened and progressive world, free, it was believed, of the Old World encumbrances and dependencies that frustrate human aspirations. As a consequence of the Revolution, a segment of the periphery has become a core.

How fully or feebly the hopes and ideals of the American Revolution have been fulfilled is another matter, as is the question of whether this form of sudden, hyperidealistic emergence is better than a gradual, more controlled evolution. But however one judges these modes of emergence from colonial status to independence, they are different, and they have left deep and different impressions on subsequent history.

The Search for Perfection

Atlantic Dimensions

It is an honor to address the British Academy, especially in any association with Isaiah Berlin. I knew him only slightly, but I recall vividly my first encounter with him. Students at Harvard in the late 1940s had been exposed to some remarkable lecturers from abroad: Joseph Schumpeter, Hans Kohn, Erwin Panofsky. But none of them prepared me for the experience of Isaiah Berlin's lectures. Words, ideas, references, allusions came in floods. It was overwhelming. I quickly realized, as I listened, that while I was intensely interested in his announced subject, I had no idea what he was talking about—and would have none, until I drove my own intensity level to somewhere within his range. We listened to this Paganini of the platform, as Michael Oakeshott called him, and observed him, with awe.[1]

But at the same time, Berlin was listening to us and observing us, with something quite a bit less than awe. And upon his return to England he wrote a three-part commentary on his experiences at Harvard, and through Harvard with the American university world in general.

He liked the students, he said. They were "more intellectually curious, more responsive to every influence, more deeply and immediately charmed by everything new . . . and above all, endowed with a quality of moral vitality unlike any I had found anywhere else." But he had also to say that "many of these excellent young people could not, as a general rule, either read or write, as these activities are understood in our best universities. That is to say, their thoughts came higglety-pigglety out of the big, buzzing, booming confusion of their minds, too many pouring out chaotically in the same instant."

But there was a deeper problem. Harvard was an academic community, he wrote, "painfully aware of the social and economic miseries of their society":

> A student or professor in this condition wonders whether it can be right for him to absorb himself in the study of, let us say, the early Greek epic . . . while the poor of south Boston go hungry and unshod and negroes are denied fundamental rights.

He had suggested to his students that intellectual curiosity was not necessarily a form of sin, and that it was valid to pursue some branch of knowledge simply because one was interested in it. But that, they seemed to think, was a European point of view, rather exotic and perhaps slightly sinister. He had pondered all this and concluded that "this naive, sincere and touching morality, according to which . . . the primary duty of everyone is to help others . . . with no indication of what it is to help others to be or do" was leading to a view of the world as "an enormous hospital of which all men are inmates, with the obligation of acting as nurses and physicians to one another." How, in such a world, he asked, could disinterested study flourish and the potentialities of mind and sensibility unfold?[2]

This was, and has been, the central paradox and energizing dynamic of higher education and scholarship in America. Analyzing the early Greek epic while attempting to improve the lives of the poor—this duality of purpose has lain at the heart of the institutions of higher education in America from the beginning, from that critical, bitterly contested passage in the late seventeenth and early eighteenth centuries when Harvard College's self-governing Fellows, modeled on their counterparts in the colleges of England's ancient universities, were transformed from an internal self-directing body of scholars and teachers to an external board of laymen whose charge it was to see that the College lived up to its public responsibilities.[3] We were then, as institutions, and still are, devoted to both society's needs and the subtleties of the early

Greek epic. The duality arises from sources deep within American society—its pragmatism, its pluralism, its constant reinvention. It is a theme that echoes through three centuries of American history.

There are other themes of similar importance and antiquity in American history, some of peculiar interest to Berlin, and none more central to his view of the world and its turmoils than the search for perfection.

This was a subject that went to the core of Berlin's defense of "the liberal anticommunist position in the midst of the Cold War."[4] His comments on the dangers of perfectionism had begun with his discussion of positive liberty in his famous inaugural lecture, "Two Concepts of Liberty," at Oxford in 1958. While at times, he then wrote, it might be justifiable "to coerce men in the name of some goal (let us say, justice or public health) which they would, if they were more enlightened, themselves pursue," once one claims that one knows what others need better than they know it themselves, one is "in a position to ignore the actual wishes of men or societies, to bully, oppress, torture them in the name, and on behalf of their 'real' selves . . . albeit often submerged and inarticulate."

It was a theme to which he returned again and again, elaborately in "The Decline of Utopian Ideas in the West" in 1978, eloquently in "The Pursuit of the Ideal" in 1988. The pursuit of perfection, he then wrote—thirty years after "Two Concepts"—was "a recipe for bloodshed, no better even if it is demanded by the sincerest of idealists, the purest of heart."[5] The implications of this position were immense, and he was challenged from the ideological right and left, as well as from the philosophical center. But the majority of informed opinion supported him in denouncing utopianism as the ideological source of modern totalitarianism and in describing the horrors that perfectionists of various kinds have wrought.[6]

As he reached back through Western history to trace the origins and different formulations of the idea of perfection that had culminated in the crushing tyrannies of the twentieth century, Berlin thought, as always, in terms of formal discourses—texts worthy of logical analysis. For he was, in this as in all his major historical writing, a historian of ideas as only a philosopher, however nonpracticing, could be. It was the structure of ideas, their genealogies, and their implications and ramifications that chiefly interested him. It was the master thinkers among the perfectionists who mattered, their cogent, fully developed texts that deserved analysis, not the often muddled and always eclectic derivatives that were part of everyday culture.

Yet it is perfectionism at that lower level—unoriginal, derivative, sometimes confused, often passionate, muddling together diverse notions and attitudes to compose guides for action—that I wish to discuss, and to suggest that at that more colloquial level there lies an earlier history of perfectionism that reveals not sources of human devastation in the search for perfection, but hope and heightened aspirations—a premodern era in which, as Quentin Skinner has written, positive liberty was "a dream, not a nightmare."[7] And further, I wish to suggest that the profound strain of perfectionism that runs through the culture of early modern Europe has a peculiar relationship to what we now think of as Atlantic history.

For it was in the seemingly unconstrained amplitudes of the Western Hemisphere and not in Europe's tightly meshed social environment, where establishments forced the expression of such yearnings into narrow interstices, that the search for perfection could find practical fulfillment in shaping the lives of ordinary people. It was there that perfectionist aspirations could fully dilate, and expanded visions could be projected into what Keith Thomas has called "action-oriented" utopias.[8]

Perfectionist thinking is a subject of some complexity if only because it has taken so many forms. It includes humanistic literary utopianism, prophetic millenarianism, and mystical hermeticism. They are complex in themselves, and they are not wholly distinct. Nothing important in the culture of early modern Christian Europe and America was solely secular. More's *Utopia* was fresh in most literate minds in the sixteenth and seventeenth centuries, but so too were the prophecies of Daniel and the dark complexities of the Book of Revelation. Keith Thomas lists eight forms of utopianism in seventeenth-century England but finds that they cannot be distinguished from the millenarian impulse, "which relied on divine inter- vention and envisaged a miraculous transformation of both man and nature. . . . [I]t was precisely when the millenarian current was running most strongly," he writes, "that the utopian faith in human effort was most buoyant." Seventeenth-century millenarianism and seventeenth-century utopianism, he concludes, "were twins."[9]

And so they were throughout the whole of early modern Europe, impelled by the power of the Ref- ormation and the vast efflorescence of knowledge in the Renaissance and beyond. Both created soaring hopes for the transcendence of life as it was known, ultimately for the possibility if not of reaching per- fection, then of approaching ideal goals.

England in the crisis years of the mid-seventeenth century was especially alight with projects for both mobilizing secular knowledge in learned and benev- olent societies, often in collaboration with the most imaginative scholars and scientists of Europe, and for advancing apocalyptic hopes. "Virtually every sect,"

Frank and Fritzie Manuel write in their history of utopian thought in Europe,

> carried its own utopia, and individuals moved easily from one circle into another, punctuating their advent and departure with an appropriate religious revelation. Men dropped in and out of groups, recanting previous errors, writing confessions and testimonials [as one radical sect sought] to distinguish itself from the teeming mass, and much energy was expended on touting the superiority of one future society over its rivals.

Some utopian designs were lofty abstractions, theoretical models of the ideal by which to measure the evils of the world and speculations on radical reform in all spheres of life. But others seemed to be within the reach of possibility. Most of these, on the Continent as in England, were the work of sects determined to recover a lost Christian perfection by drawing apart to live more perfect lives in some approximation to the assumed ways of the apostles.

Often the radical sectarians found the social atmosphere of their immediate localities too dense, the weight of traditional institutions and social controls too heavy to allow for local withdrawal. So they looked for refuge beyond their immediate horizons, some to distant transoceanic places, and in this they shared the visions of the humanist utopian theorists for whom imagined distances from the real world had always been a logical necessity, often involving fanciful ocean voyages to reach the perfectly imagined regime.[10]

For both, America's attraction was powerful. Not only would its limitless spaces and apparent lack of restrictive social pressures provide the ideal environment for the pursuit of perfectionist lives, but the existence of its vast population of pagans, descendants no doubt of the lost tribes of Israel, now Satan's captives, would provide the ultimate challenge for those who understood the stages of apocalyptic fulfillment. And so the perfectionist invasion began—by Catholics, by dissenting Anglicans, by German pietists, and by a range of radical Protestants, from self-absorbed seekers to those wildly impatient Fifth Monarchy militants, led by a murderous New England "fanatique," who stormed through Restoration London crying, "Live King Jesus!" until rounded up and hanged.[11]

Utopian and perfectionist aspirations were an elemental part of the European invasion of the Americas. The conquest—by the English, Dutch, French, and Portuguese as well as by the Spanish—was barbarous for the conquerors, and for the natives catastrophic. Yet amid all the racist brutality, the loss of civility, and the remorseless, often bloody struggles to create new economic and social regimes, the search for perfection and for the fulfillment of apocalyptic prophecies—impulses that flowed from Europe's heartland—persisted. Certain passages in this complex multicultural history are particularly revealing. They exemplify something of the inner landscape of the European imagination and America's peculiar place within it.

The Spanish were first on the scene. For the early Franciscans, led by the ascetic Toribio Motolinía, who was convinced that America could be nothing less than the prime site of the millennial kingdom of Christ, the task was to help the natives recover the simplicity and innocence he believed they had lost in the Aztecs' conquest. Once, in earlier, pre-Aztec times, they had been free of luxury, greed, and the struggle for "rank and honors." If that pristine world could be revived, the Indians, in their innocence, would occupy "a primordial, privileged role at the center itself of the future of humanity." Motolinía lectured Charles V on the urgent need to "hasten the hour of the Final Judgment," not by imposing modern Hispanic culture on the natives but by protecting them from all outside influences except Christian preaching, which could rightly be imposed by force.[12]

Though he wrote at length and with passion,

Motolinía failed to convince the crown to protect the Indians' autochthonous cultures. So the aggressive Hispanization proceeded, in innumerable missions, churches, and schools throughout the viceroyalties, creating in the process an auspicious background for specific utopian designs.

They appeared in different forms at different places. Some were newly invented, others drawn from classic sources. More's *Utopia* was understood in humanist circles to be a learned, imaginative, and challenging commentary on Europe's ills; but in America it had practical consequences. For the *audiencia* judge and later bishop Vasco de Quiroga, it provided a detailed model for the organizational structure and social discipline of the *pueblo*-hospitals he founded near Mexico City in the early 1530s. The specific provisions for these benevolent, perfectionist communities, built to shelter and care for the poor, vagrant, and dispossessed Indians, could not have been closer to the details of More's imaginative design. Property was owned in common, the basic social unit was the *familia,* work was limited to six hours a day, goods were distributed according to need, luxury and useless offices were eliminated, and judges were elected by families. Quiroga even considered a dress code based on *Utopia,* including clothes of fabrics specified by More. The organization of More's *Utopia,* Quiroga wrote, should be the basis not only of his hospitals but of all Indian communities in America.

More's utopian model, a literary text, had become "a political program circulated across the Atlantic from a radical colonist to a monarch and used to initiate a social practice."[13] But for others, equally committed to ideal goals, there were no models, literary or other, and pragmatic solutions had to be found. So the Spanish Jesuits devised "reductions" of the natives, in Paraguay most famously but elsewhere as well. They too were millenarian/utopian creations: gatherings of nomadic natives into disciplined urban communities where Christianity, hence civilization, could be inculcated in people who would thereafter become productive members of the labor force and foot soldiers in the wars of imperial expansion.

But the Indians the Portuguese Jesuits faced in Brazil and the Iroquois and Hurons the French Jesuits faced in New France could not be forced, in Berlin's phrase, "into neat uniforms demanded by the dogmatically believed-in schemes." The indigenous cultures were too vibrant to be easily uprooted and the power of the invaders was too weak to force the natives into an ideal mold shaped by perfectionist visions. The Jesuits' wards never fully abandoned their native cultures. They absorbed the new regimes selectively, forcing their rulers, if only for the sake of stability, to accept major aspects of the indigenous organizations.[14]

The search for perfection in these forms, on the background of millenarian hopes for the redemption of the Western world, was a transoceanic projection of the apocalyptic prophecies that gripped the European imagination and the associated yearnings for a return to the simplicity of the primitive church. As such it was as much French, Dutch, and German as it was Spanish and Portuguese. And above all it was English.

There is no better illustration of the spatial dimensions of the search for perfection than the fortunes of the Puritans who, fleeing from ecclesiastical oppression at home, sought to establish in America a model of perfected Christianity. Everything seemed to favor their success. They had sufficient numbers and funds, administrative experience, and some of England's finest scholars and theologians who shared a passionate belief that they were building in Massachusetts God's "new Jerusalem," laying "one stone in the foundacion of this new Syon." The "great persons" of his grandparents' generation, wrote Cotton Mather, who like Guillaume Budé had "mistook Sir Thomas Moor's UTOPIA for a country really existent, and stirr'd up some divines charitably to undertake a voyage thither, might now have certainly found a truth in their mistake; New England was a true Utopia."[15]

But however utopian in aspiration, the Puritans did not have a unified belief in what the perfected church and society should be, and so immediately upon landing, their community, boiling with perfectionist ambitions, exploded, "hurling itself outward to its ultimate limits." Perfectionist groups left and right fought for domination. Antinomians denounced the unconverted clergy as "dead dogs" and tore the colony apart with their repudiation of ascetic discipline as they moved toward mystical union with God. Rationalist Socinians settled in villages a hundred miles inland from Boston declared that the Trinity, atonement, and the divinity of Christ were delusions and argued for religious toleration. And Anabaptists, scattered everywhere, insisted that infant baptism was a deadly corruption, to which conservatives replied by invoking memories of Münster, where, a century earlier, zealous Anabaptists had been slaughtered by the thousands by those, including Luther, who feared anarchic upheavals.[16]

But New England was no Münster. Its open spaces, social and geographical, invited the free, limitless expression of the many perfectionist impulses that lurked in the heart of Puritanism—not only antinomianism, socinianism, and anabaptism but familism, spiritism, and those nameless ecstatic urges that would become notorious and deadly when proclaimed by Ranters in London but that in Rhode Island, a colony that the mainstream Puritans denounced as "a cesspool of vile heresies and irreligion," found free institutional form. There, each of the various perfectionist villages, led by its own self-styled "professor of the mysteries of Christ," was convinced of its purity and condemned its errant neighbors. All felt an irresistible pressure to press on through deepening stages to reach some ultimate, uncompromised, perfect resolution—a state of being that Roger Williams alone, finally, attained.[17]

Williams, the purest of Puritan perfectionists, began his career as a spiritual guide to Cromwell's aunt, the melancholic Lady Joan Barrington, whom he so berated for the unsatisfactory state of her soul that she banished him from her sight. The same "unlambe-like . . . stiffnesse" led him to join the migration to Boston, and then to quit Boston after denouncing the Puritans' failure to separate fully from the corrupt Church of England, their union of church and state, the "Soule-rape" of their "forcing of the conscience of any person," and their immoral seizing of Indian lands. Narrowly escaping deportation to England, he fled to the woods near Narragansett Bay where, with a small troop of followers, he formed his more perfect village.[18]

But not perfect enough. There was no stopping in his fiercely logical pursuit of the ultimate form of apostolic purity. Convinced that there could be no "true Church until Christ himself reinstituted it at the end of time," he swept through and discarded layer after layer of recognized doctrines until nothing was left but his own elemental convictions based on his millenarian view of Christian history. Since no post-apostolic church was true, no church should be joined, and so in the end Williams became a church unto himself, worshipping alone, or with his wife, in what he took to be the only true approximation of apostolic form, and sending back to England from his bayside refuge bulletins of his beliefs and blistering attacks on his enemies' and the world's corruptions.[19]

But it was the Reverend John Eliot, of all the millenarian missionaries, who drew the most radically utopian and institutionally elaborate prescriptions from the common, pan-European sources. It was Eliot who sought most efficiently to relate the conversion of the natives to the future of mankind.

Eliot, not the most learned of the Puritan preachers, though he was said to have arrived in America with twenty-three barrels of books, had begun in the 1640s to reach out to the Indians to urge them to lead Christian lives and eventually to find true faith. Then two events coincided to elevate his mission to cosmic heights and to enclose within a single vision the perfectionist destinies of the Indians and the fulfillment of the millenarian prophecies.

In a series of lectures in the 1640s, Boston's leading

theologian, John Cotton, discoursed vividly on the twenty-two chapters of the Book of Revelation, leaving a searing impression on Eliot that the predestined end of history was approaching and that the entire drama of Christ's deliverance would soon be enacted, with all its momentous transformations. Then came the execution of Charles I, which could only be seen as the unmistakable first step in the prophesied destruction of all earthly monarchies and the presage of the rule of Christ. A new, millenarian polity was now required, and it would be extrapolated from the small-scale model that he, Eliot, would create among the Indians in New England. They would be "reduced" to civility by being gathered from their wanderings into settled towns. There, governed by elected rulers of tens, of fifties, of hundreds, and of thousands as prescribed in Exodus 18, they would be able to lead perfected Christian lives within covenanted churches, in preparation for Christ's deliverance.[20]

For Eliot the praying Indian towns, of which fourteen were established by 1675, bore heavily on the destiny of mankind. "I doubt not," he wrote to Cromwell, "but it will be some comfort to your heart, to see the kingdom of Christ rising up in these western parts of the world, a blessed kingdom that will in time 'fill all the earth.'" In his *Christian Commonwealth, or the Civil Polity of the Rising Kingdom of Jesus Christ,* written

in 1651 at the height of his apocalyptic fervor, Eliot
laid out the full vision of the project among the Indians that gripped his imagination. With the praying
towns epitomes of what could prevail in England—
a nation, he believed, that was destined to be one of
the two inaugural locations of the millennium (the
other being New England)—and given the likelihood
that the Indians, "ripe for utopian molding," were
descendants of the lost tribes of Israel, their conversion, followed by that of all gentiles, would indicate
that the kingdom of Christ was nigh.[21]

Eliot sought to realize in utopian communities in
America ideas drawn from major themes in European
culture and then to transfer their embodied form back
across the Atlantic to serve as templates for the radical transformation of England. But his message and
the reports of his praying towns reached an England
in turmoil over the proper form of republican government. His urgent advice was taken to mean that
England should give up ransacking law, history, and
constitutional theory to find proper forms of government and draw on scripture alone, for, he wrote,
"Christ is your King and Soveraign Lawgiver," "the
only right heir to the crown of England." England's
constitution should, like the Indians', consist of elected
rulers of tens, fifties, hundreds, and thousands, with
suffrage for all self-sufficient males. This, he wrote, is

the form of government, infinitely expandable, "by which Christ meaneth to rule all the nations on earth according to Scriptures."[22]

It was a perfect scheme for a perfect Christian regime, but the world was not prepared for his perfection. Eliot's praying Indian towns were wiped out in the savage Indian war of 1675–76, their eleven hundred inhabitants exiled to a harbor island where many starved or died of disease. And his prophetic book, delayed in publication until the year before the Restoration, proved to be a deadly embarrassment to the Massachusetts authorities, promoting as it did Fifth Monarchy views that would surely bring down on the colony the wrath of the restored royal government. They forthwith collected and destroyed every copy of the book they could lay their hands on and forced Eliot to recant everything in it.[23]

As in some bewilderment he did so, perfectionist impulses were evolving elsewhere—in Holland and the scattered German states—that would be fulfilled in British North America. One of the most fully developed schemes designed to begin the world's reformation emerged from Amsterdam, and specifically from the heated atmosphere of the poets and freethinkers who gathered at that city's Sweet Rest Tavern. It too would run its course through Atlantic networks. The designer and spiritual leader of this utopian program was a visionary Dutchman, Pieter Cornelisz Plockhoy, who had been touched as a child in Zeeland by the fierce Biblicism and spirituality of the Mennonites and Anabaptists and as a young man had found inspiration among the Quaker-like "Collegiant" philosophers in Amsterdam, devoted to absolute religious freedom and social justice. There he had begun his search for "the ideal Christian commonwealth of love, equality, and freedom." By the mid-1650s he had made contact with the famous German-Polish virtuoso of radical reform, Samuel Hartlib, then in London, and through him with the circle of erudite pansophists seeking to mobilize and employ all human knowledge to reform everything—from politics to agriculture, from employment to "the spirits of men," and from commerce and poverty to law and the arts.[24]

For Plockhoy, the Hartlib circle, devoted to recovering "man's lost dominion over nature" and to transforming life as it was known, was irresistible. Abandoning family and home, he joined Hartlib, and with his help gained access to Cromwell. The great man, Plockhoy said, listened "several times with patience" to his ideas and proposals, which by then had taken elaborate form.[25]

Plockhoy knew exactly what the perfect world should be. It would have "freedom of speech, absolute toleration, and a universal Christianity." There would be no clergy, no ties of church to state, no tithes, and above all, no "lording over consciences." The thralldom brought on by malevolent governors, greedy merchants, and lazy ministers would be eliminated. Life's work would be shared in clear divisions of labor; specialization would bring interdependence and mutual respect. There would be absolute equality of status; property would be held in common until divided by lot into private parcels. Above all it would be a full-employment welfare society in which the health and well-being of all people would be provided for. As to the controversial issue of equality, "nobody will be so naïve," he wrote, "much less malevolent, as to think . . . that we are attempting to remove all differences among people." The effect of the common rules would be to eliminate not natural human differences nor rewards for personal accomplishments but the differences created and maintained by force and intimidation, by the dead hand of custom, and by the coercive mandates of the princes of the church.[26]

Such was the program Plockhoy presented to Cromwell, and after his death to the new Protector and to Parliament. Its aim, he said, was the true reformation of England as the first step in the rebirth of mankind. If in England complete religious freedom were created, he assured Cromwell, "Holland, Denmark, Sweden, France and other kingdoms . . . will easily be brought to a firm bond of unity."[27]

But while his proposals stirred up much talk and

some writing, there was little action. Plockhoy's thinking began to shift. In England, he wrote, it was becoming clear that he and his adherents might well prove to be "insufferable to the world," and at the same time the world might be "incorrigible or unbetterable as to us." Therefore he and his people would have to establish their solidarity "in such places as are separate from other men, where we may with less impediment or hindrance love one another and mind the wonders of God, eating the bread we shall earn with our own hands."[28]

But where could such a refuge be found? The authorities in his native Holland turned him away, and he had no confidence in what he heard of a nobleman's sanctuary near Cologne. In the end, well aware that the Hartlib circle had talked of creating an ideal society ("Antilia," "Macaria") in Virginia or Bermuda, he decided that his perfect society would only be safe, and fulfilled, in America. He knew about that distant land through his brother who had served the Dutch West India Company in New Netherland and from a member of the Parnassan Club who had lived there for a decade and who celebrated its wonders in rhapsodic poems which he declaimed at length to his friends in the Sweet Rest Tavern.[29]

For this removal to their underpopulated colony the Dutch West India Company and the Amsterdam authorities were happy to provide support. So on

July 28, 1663, Plockhoy and forty-one adherents dis-
embarked at an abandoned clearing on the Delaware
River, to usher in a new era in human history.

What happened within Plockhoy's perfect world
in the months that followed, how fully and in what
detail he was able finally, on that distant shore, to realize his so carefully defined state of perfected being, is
not known. What is known is that it ended swiftly. In
August 1664 an overwhelming English force seized the
Dutch colony and swept across Plockhoy's settlement
like a whirlwind, stripping it bare and plundering it
down "to a very nail." Plockhoy died in the attack or
soon thereafter and his utopian flock scattered among
the Finnish, Swedish, German, and English frontiers-
men living in primitive settlements alongside the
Lenape Indians. Only his blind son is known to have
survived into the next century, the last remnant of
the utopia that had once stirred the minds of aspir-
ing intellectuals in Holland and learned pansophists in
England and the German states.[30]

But if one utopian mission born in the heated
atmosphere of European perfectionism failed on the
banks of the Delaware River, others drawn from different sources appeared nearby.

William Penn's private colony, founded in 1681 as
a refuge for harassed Quakers committed to their own
militant struggle for perfection, was open to people
of all nations and (Protestant) creeds. It was quickly

peopled not only by Welsh and English sectarians but also by German Protestants from the Rhineland and the Palatinate. Victims of the ravages of war and of religious persecution, most were members of established Lutheran and Reformed churches. But among them were small groups of radical perfectionists with different aims, disciples of the major figures in German Pietism: Spener, Boehme, and Francke. One such group, who called themselves the Chapter of Perfection, put together a program drawn from cabalist, Rosicrucian, and biblical sources that had allowed them to predict the arrival of Christ and the start of the millennium precisely in 1694. Confident of the accuracy of their textual analyses, their mathematical calculations, and the meaning of the revelations they had received, they were properly disposed, according to their androgynous theology, to accept in ecstasy the embrace of the Bridegroom when he arrived.[31]

So the Chapter of Perfection, under the leadership of Johannes Kelpius, both a Rosicrucian magus and a *magister* of the University of Altdorf, set out for Pennsylvania to prepare for the coming of the Lord and to seek that state of personal perfection that was free of all sensuous temptations and beyond all rational understanding. Quickly upon their arrival they built a log-walled monastery of perfect proportions: forty feet by forty feet. It had a common room for communal worship and also cells where the celibate brethren could search for personal perfection by contemplating their magic numbers and their esoteric symbols. In a primitive laboratory they conducted alchemical and pharmaceutical experiments aimed at eliminating disease and prolonging life indefinitely. And on the roof they placed a telescope, which they manned from dusk till dawn, so that in case the Bridegroom came in the middle of the night they would be prepared to receive him. But the heart of Kelpius's sect lay not in the common room, not in the cells, and not in the laboratory, but in a cave which the magus found in a nearby hillside and in which he pondered truths concealed to ordinary souls but revealed to him by signs, by symbols, by numbers, and by pure contemplation. Everything confirmed that it was here, in the Chapter of Perfection, that the "dear Lord Jesus" would reveal himself and that all true Christians, while vigorously pursuing their own perfection, should await him and prepare for the heavenly feast.

When the year passed and the Bridegroom failed to appear, calculations were renewed, the contemplation of numbers and symbols was intensified, and trancelike states were repeated. But gradually the brethren's discipline weakened, their energy dissipated, and temptation drew them from their celibate state. Some defected to established churches, but others went off to more recent perfectionist sects that were multiplying across Penn's province. Few could tolerate the fierce self-mortifying discipline required in Johann Beissel's nearby Ephrata cloister, whose emaciated monks and nuns sought, through the demanding rites of the Rosicrucians, to achieve a higher, more perfect state of being.[32] More genial were the followers of Matthias Baumann, an ignorant laborer from Lambsheim, in the Palatinate, who believed that in the delirium of an illness he had been transported to heaven where, newborn, purged of all sin, he had attained perfection and needed thereafter no intervention of church, sacraments, or any other means of grace. He was convinced that God dwelt in him as in Christ ("we are brothers," he said) and that he had become like Adam before the Fall, incapable of sin—conditions he extended to his followers and which he urged the unregenerate to achieve. When some questioned the truth of his doctrine of perfection, he proposed to demonstrate his exalted state by walking across the surface of the Delaware River. And there was an array of semicommunistic Moravian settlements, fugitive groups of the Czech-Saxon *Unitas Fratrum*, which spawned dozens of obscure, short-lived utopias deep in Indian territory.[33]

For two centuries perfectionist projects, plants of European origins, had blossomed in the open atmosphere of the Americas, had reached for the sun, and had faded and died. But they were not without lasting effect. Their creative influence can be found deep in the cultures of later times.

New England Puritanism's once explosive radicalism was compromised into a sere orthodoxy, but Roger Williams's uncompromised perfectionism, feared and despised by his contemporaries, proved in the twentieth century to be an inspiration for advocates of religious freedom, human rights, and enlightened democracy. Eliot's passions were stifled and his efforts to convert and educate the natives and to modernize their way of life led to cultural deracination, but his translation of the Bible into Massachusett, "the first printed in a non-European tongue, and the first printed for which an entire phonetic writing system was devised," together with his tracts in the natives' language and his *Indian Grammar,* contributed significantly to the development of Indian linguistics in the nineteenth and twentieth centuries.[34]

Plockhoy's communal utopia was wiped out, but his ideas were not. Adopted by the Quaker political economist John Bellers later in the century, they were transmitted through him to Robert Owen, whose radical social programs they profoundly influenced. They were thereafter incorporated into Marx's labor theory of value, cited at length by Eduard Bernstein in his revisionist writings on social democracy, endorsed

by the reformer Joshua Rowntree, and studied by
modern full-employment economists. In 1968 all of
Plockhoy's publications, Dutch and English, were
translated into French as appendices to a treatise on
Plockhoy's cooperative utopianism and Christian ecu-
menism published by the École Pratique des Hautes
Études.[35] And if Kelpius's Chapter of Perfection
quickly disappeared, the spirit of German Pietism did
not, and produced enduring communities of Mennonites, Amish, Dunkards, and Schwenkfelders. Even
Matthias Baumann's hallucinatory perfectionism had
important consequences: it helped inspire the many
"holiness revivals" of the nineteenth century and left
traces in modern American evangelicalism.[36]

The search for perfection, generated in Europe's vortex, when played out in the spatial amplitudes of the
West, was the source not of monstrous tyrannies but
of spiritual and moral striving. It did not become the
"recipe for bloodshed" that Berlin so feared because
everywhere it lacked the ultimate power to coerce.
Utopianism, secular or religious, becomes a "road
to inhumanity" when it is enforced by a monopoly
of power—ultimate, unconstrained power in whatever form it might appear: the repressive power of
the Soviet state, the annihilatory power of the Nazi
regime, the mind-blinding power of Maoist gangs,

the suffocating power of Islamic fundamentalism, each of which emerged through distinctive historical circumstances, to seek by violence what could not be achieved by persuasion.

Did Berlin not know this? In some sense of course he did. "Two Concepts" was formally cast as a discourse on the permissible limits of coercion; "force" and "constraint" are repeatedly referred to, and Berlin denied that all historical conflicts are reducible to conflicts of ideas. But political concepts, he believed, when not subjected to rational criticism can "acquire an unchecked momentum and an irresistible power over multitudes."[37] From his embattled position in the defense of a liberal alternative to totalitarianism, the enemy was ideological perfectionism, the passionate pursuit of which he took to be the driving force behind the twentieth century's tyrannies. No one knew better than Berlin or expressed more brilliantly the genealogy and structure of perfectionist ideas. But their threat to civilization, in the most general terms, lay not in their intrinsic malevolence but in the brutality of those who implacably imposed them: the populist thugs, the fanatical monopolists of power—beings alien to Berlin's sensibilities, incomprehensible to his humanely inquiring mind.

Appendix

With the exception of items 2, 4, and 5, the following sections were originally published and are reprinted courtesy of the sources noted below:

1. "Considering the Slave Trade: History and Memory," *William and Mary Quarterly*, 3rd ser., 58, no. 1 (January 2001), 245–52.
2. "Context in History," the Charles Joseph La Trobe Memorial Lecture in North American History, La Trobe University, Melbourne, 1995.
3. "The Challenge of Modern Historiography," *American Historical Review*, 87, no. 1 (February 1982), 1–24.
4. "History and the Creative Imagination," the Lewin Lecture, Washington University, St. Louis, 1985.
5. "The Losers: Notes on the Historiography of Loyalism," Appendix in Bernard Bailyn, *The Ordeal of Thomas Hutchinson* (Cambridge, Mass., 1974), 383–408; originally a Trevelyan Lecture, University of Cambridge, 1971.
6. "Thomas Hutchinson in Context: *The Ordeal* Revisited," *Proceedings of the American Antiquarian Society*, 114, part 2 (2006), 281–99.
7. (With John Clive) "England's Cultural Provinces: Scotland and America," *William and Mary Quarterly*, 3rd ser., 11, no. 2 (April 1954), 200–213.
8. "The Peopling of the British Peripheries in the Eighteenth Century," the Esso Lecture, the Australian Academy of the Humanities, 1988.
9. "The Search for Perfection: Atlantic Dimensions," the Isaiah Berlin Lecture, *Proceedings of the British Academy*, 151 (2007), 135–58.

Acknowledgments

I am grateful to my hosts for their hospitality on the occasions of the presentation of these essays: Professor Sir John Plumb, at the University of Cambridge; Professor David Konig, at Washington University, St. Louis; and Professor Alan Frost at La Trobe University, Melbourne—and to the sponsoring institutions: the British Academy, the Omohundro Institute of Early American History and Culture, and the American Antiquarian Society. Lotte Bailyn was a witness at all of these occasions—especially at the affectionately contentious collaboration with John Clive, which she somehow managed to keep coherent—and encouraged me to publish the results together as a book. I am grateful too to my colleagues Emma Rothschild, who was kind enough to go over and comment on an early draft, and David Holland, who kept me up to date on the Perry Miller bibliography.

Andrew Miller was a thoughtful and patient editor, who kept a critical and sympathetic eye on the development of the book. William Heyward worked patiently to see the book through production. And Jennifer Nickerson was wonderfully effective in keeping track of the various drafts, checking details, and preparing the texts and notes for publication.

Notes

I.

CONSIDERING THE SLAVE TRADE:
HISTORY AND MEMORY

All citations are to papers in *William and Mary Quarterly*, 3rd ser., 58, no. 1 (January 2001), "New Perspectives on the Transatlantic Slave Trade."

1. Lorena S. Walsh, "The Chesapeake Slave Trade: Regional Patterns, African Origins, and Some Simplifications," 139.
2. David Eltis, "The Volume and Structure of the Transatlantic Slave Trade: A Reassessment," 34, 39.
3. G. Ugo Nwokeji, "African Conceptions of Gender and the Slave Traffic," 55, 66.
4. David Richardson, "Shipboard Revolts, African Authority, and the Atlantic Slave Trade," 81, 89.
5. Herbert S. Klein, Stanley L. Engerman, Robin Haines, and Ralph Shlomowitz, "Transoceanic Mortality: The Slave Trade in Comparative Perspective," 95, 109.
6. Walsh, "Chesapeake Slave Trade," 144.
7. Stephen Behrendt, "Markets, Transaction Cycles, and Profits: Merchant Decision Making in the British Slave Trade," 201; Trevor Burnard and Kenneth Morgan, "The Dynamics of the Slave Market and Slave Purchasing Patterns in Jamaica, 1655–1788," 208, 218.
8. Burnard and Morgan, "Dynamics of the Slave Market," 211, 220.
9. Ralph A. Austen, "The Slave Trade as History and Memory: Confrontations of Slaving Voyage Documents and Communal Traditions," 231, 237.

2.

CONTEXT IN HISTORY

1. Quoted in Alan Gross, *Charles Joseph La Trobe* (Melbourne, 1956), 7.

2. Charles Joseph La Trobe, *The Rambler in North America: MDCCCXXXII–MDCCCXXXIII* (London, 1835), II, 96, 15–16, 70, 71. For an example of La Trobe's parodic but perceptive descriptions, see his passage on "the fluency of the country lawyers . . . the unhesitating delivery, command of language, and long-windedness," II, 67–68.

3. L. J. Blake, ed., *Letters of Charles Joseph La Trobe* (Victoriana Series No. 1, Melbourne, 1975); A. G. L. Shaw, ed., *Gipps–La Trobe Correspondence, 1839-1846* (Melbourne, 1989).

4. For a preliminary effort in this direction, see Bernard Bailyn and Philip D. Morgan, eds., *Strangers within the Realm: Cultural Margins of the First British Empire* (Chapel Hill, N.C., 1991).

5. Adrian Wilson and T. G. Ashplant, "Whig History and Present-Centred History," *Historical Journal,* 31 (1988), 1. This thoroughgoing critique was published in two parts: 31 (1988), 1–16; 253–73, and concluded with the thought that what Butterfield called "whiggism" is a special case of "present-centredness," which, the authors say, raises the problem of the choices historians must make about which people, aspects, and dimensions of the past to study. See also A. Rupert Hall, "On Whiggism," *History of Science,* 21 (1983), 45–59.

6. Herbert Butterfield, *The Whig Interpretation of History* (London, 1931), 29, 7, 30, 108.

7. E.g., Herbert Butterfield, "The Moderate Cupidity of Everyman," *New York Times,* January 3, 1973; "Inward to Glory," *New York Times,* January 4, 1973. For one reaction to Butterfield's pronouncements on public affairs and their relation to his historiography and religious beliefs, see Maurice Cowling,

"Herbert Butterfield 1900–1979," *Proceedings of the British Academy,* 65 (1979), 595–609.

8. Herbert Butterfield, *The Origins of Modern Science* [1957] (rev. ed., New York, 1965), 8–9, 39, 40, 43, 44, 53, 65. Newton's interest in alchemy has become a standard subject for historians of science. Karin Figala and Ulrich Petzold, "Alchemy in the Newtonian Circle . . . The Late Phase of Isaac Newton's Alchemy," in *Renaissance and Revolution,* ed. J. V. Field and Frank A. J. L. James (Cambridge, England, 1993).

9. E.g., ibid., 12–13; A. Rupert Hall, *The Revolution in Science* (London, 1983); David C. Lindberg, "Conceptions of the Scientific Revolution from Bacon to Butterfield: A Preliminary Sketch," in *Reappraisals of the Scientific Revolution,* ed. D. C. Lindberg and Robert S. Westman (Cambridge, England, 1990), xvii, 1–2, 18–19, 367, 369, 371.

10. Frances A. Yates, *The Rosicrucian Enlightenment* [1972] (Boulder, Colo., 1978), 25, 231. Cf. Brian P. Copenhaver, "Natural Magic, Hermeticism, and Occultism in Early Modern Science," in *Reappraisals of the Scientific Revolution.* It is interesting to note that Marie Boas, in her technically advanced *The Scientific Renaissance, 1450–1630* (London, 1962), published five years after Butterfield's *Origins,* does not mention that earlier, more general work.

11. Keith Thomas, *Religion and the Decline of Magic* (London, 1971), 663.

12. Of the many responses Freud made to Fliess's theories, those pertaining to Fliess's notions of periodicity are particularly interesting for their careful balance between respect and doubt. See esp. *The Complete Letters of Sigmund Freud and Wilhelm Fliess, 1887–1904,* ed. and trans. Jeffrey M. Masson (Cambridge, Mass., 1985), 174, 282. On the devastating reception (or nonreception) of Freud's *Interpretation of Dreams,* see Ernest Jones, *The Life and Work of Sigmund Freud* (New York, 1953–57), I, 361.

13. Robert Darnton, *The Literary Underground of the Old Regime* (Cambridge, Mass., 1982), 39–40.

14. James Tully, ed., *Meaning and Context: Quentin Skinner and His Critics* (Oxford, 1988), 29, 59, 9, 101, 102; John Patrick Diggins, "The Oyster and the Pearl: The Problem of Contextualism in Intellectual History," *History and Theory*, 23 (1984), 151–69.

15. For one version of the swarming discussion of republicanism and liberalism, typically focusing on Louis Hartz and something called "consensus history," see Daniel T. Rodgers, "Republicanism: The Career of a Concept," *Journal of American History*, 19 (1992), 11–38. For excellent discussions of the crucial and controversial role of interpretations of American Revolutionary ideology in understanding American constitutional law and the Founders' "original intent" in writing the Constitution, see Laura Kalman, *The Strange Career of Legal Liberalism* (New Haven, Conn., 1996), chap. 4, and Jack N. Rakove, *Original Meanings: Politics and Ideas in the Making of the Constitution* (New York, 1996).

16. Bernard Bailyn, *Ideological Origins of the American Revolution* (Enlarged ed., Cambridge, Mass., 1992).

17. Michael Zuckerman, "The Power of Blackness: Thomas Jefferson and the Revolution in St. Domingue," in Zuckerman, *Almost Chosen People* (Berkeley, Calif., 1993), 215, 217, 218, 196; Michael Lind, *The Next American Nation* (New York, 1995), 369–71. Cf. Bernard Bailyn, "Jefferson and the Ambiguities of Freedom," *Proceedings of the American Philosophical Society*, 137 (1993), 498–515, quotation at 507n.

18. Herbert Butterfield, *The Englishman and His History* [1944] (Archon ed., Camden, Conn., 1970), [i], ii, 222; Brendan Bradshaw, "Nationalism and Historical Scholarship in Modern Ireland," *Irish Historical Studies*, 26 (1989), 347.

19. Brendan Bradshaw, "The Invention of the Irish," *Times Literary Supplement*, October 14, 1997, 8; Roy Foster, " 'We Are All Revisionists Now,' " *Irish Review*, 1 (1986), 1–5 (ending, "And to say 'revisionist' should just be another way of saying

historian"); Aidan Clarke, "Ireland and the General Crisis," *Past and Present*, 48 (1970), 89, 99. For a survey of the historiography of Ireland, explaining the background of the current controversies and the emergence of "a new interpretation of Irish history as a complex and ambivalent process rather than a morality tale," see Roy Foster, "History and the Irish Question," *Transactions of the Royal Historical Society*, 5th ser., 33 (1983), 169–92. For a sense of the character of the debate, see "Nationalist Perspectives on the Past: A Symposium," *Irish Review,* 4 (1988), 15–39 (Desmond Fennell, author of *The Revision of Irish Nationalism* [1989], quoted 24–25); Bradshaw, "Nationalism and Historical Scholarship," 329–51, building on Stephen G. Ellis, "Nationalist Historiography and the English and Gaelic Worlds in the Late Middle Ages," ibid., 25 (1986), 1–18; and the rebuttals and counter-rebuttals that followed Bradshaw's piece in the *Times Literary Supplement* cited above. Aidan Clarke's interpretation lies at the core of the revisionists' normalization of the Ulster rising of 1641. Thus: "It was not, as popular mythology and the 1916 Proclamation have it, one of a series of assertions by the Irish people of their right to national freedom and sovereignty, nor was it simply a sequel to the plantation in Ulster, a final attempt to reverse the Elizabethan conquest and the Jacobean settlement." Peter Roebuck, ed., *Plantation to Partition* (Belfast, 1981), 42. Cf. Clarke's "The 1641 Rebellion and Anti-Popery in Ireland," in *Ulster 1641,* ed. Brian Mac Cuarta (Belfast, 1993), 192: "the repression beloved of nineteenth-century nationalists was as much a myth as was the vision of the golden age which supposedly preceded colonisation."

20. A. J. P. Taylor, *The Origins of the Second World War* [1961] (New York, 1983), xxviii, xi.
21. John A. Garraty, "The New Deal, National Socialism, and the Great Depression," *American Historical Review,* 78 (1973), 907–44.
22. Frank Crowley, Alan D. Gilbert, K. S. Inglis, and Peter

Spearitt, general eds. (each volume has its own editors), *Australians: A Historical Library,* 11 vols., and a separate *Guide and Index* (Broadway, N.S.W., 1987); Graeme Davison, "Slicing Australian History: Reflections on the Bicentennial History Project," *New Zealand Journal of History,* 16 (1982), 7.

23. Ibid., 12, 13, 15, 11.

3.

THREE TRENDS IN MODERN HISTORY

1. Gordon Wright, "History as a Moral Science," *American Historical Review,* 81 (1976), 1.
2. Oscar Handlin, "The Capacity of Quantitative History," *Perspectives in American History,* 9 (1975), 7–26, expanded in Handlin, *Truth in History* (Cambridge, Mass., 1979), chap. 8; David Herlihy, "Numerical and Formal Analysis in European History," *Journal of Interdisciplinary History,* 12 (1981), 115–19.
3. R. A. Butlin, ed., *The Development of the Irish Town* (London, 1977), chap. 3; Gerald L. Soliday, "Marburg in Upper Hesse: A Research Report," *Journal of Family History,* 2 (1977), 164–68; Mack Walker, *German Home Towns: Community, State, and General Estate, 1648–1871* (Ithaca, N.Y., 1971); Étienne François, "Unterschichten und Armut in rheinischen Residenzstädten des 18. Jahrhunderts," *Vierteljahrschrift für Sozial- und Wirtschaftsgeschichte,* 62 (1975), 433–64; Olwen Hufton, *The Poor of Eighteenth-Century France, 1750–1789* (Oxford, 1974); Alice Hanson Jones, *Wealth of a Nation to Be: The American Colonies on the Eve of the Revolution* (New York, 1980); on the circulation and reception of Beccaria's essay, see note 9, below.
4. See below, Essay 7.
5. Fynes Moryson, *An Itinerary* (London, 1617), as quoted in David Quinn, *The Elizabethans and the Irish* (Ithaca, N.Y., 1996), 122 (italics added).
6. J. G. A. Pocock, "British History: A Plea for a New Subject,"

Journal of Modern History, 47 (1975), 601–21. Cf. Michael Hechter, *Internal Colonialism: The Celtic Fringe in British National Development, 1536–1966* (London, 1975), and the exchange of views between Pocock and Hechter following Pocock's article, 626–28.

7. Samuel Johnson, *A Journey to the Western Islands of Scotland,* ed. Mary Lascelles (New Haven, Conn., 1971), 94–99, 131.

8. William I. Hull, *Benjamin Furly and Quakerism in Rotterdam* (Swarthmore, Pa., 1941), and *William Penn and the Dutch Quaker Migration to Pennsylvania* (Swarthmore, Pa., 1935), esp. 328–45; Philip D. Curtin, *Economic Change in Precolonial Africa: Senegambia in the Era of the Slave Trade* (Madison, Wis., 1975), chaps. 2–4.

9. Much of the argument of Franco Venturi's five-volume *Settecento riformatore* (Turin, 1969–79), which traces the spread of Enlightenment ideas throughout the Western world, is summarized in his *Utopia and Reform in the Enlightenment* (Cambridge, England, 1971) and in his "Church and Reform in Enlightenment Italy: The Sixties of the Eighteenth Century," *Journal of Modern History,* 48 (1976), 215–32. His edition of Beccaria's treatise reprints the work itself in 104 pages and then presents as a 547-page appendix a documentary history of the origins of the book in Milan and its reception in Italy, France, England, Spain, Switzerland, Austria, Germany, Denmark, Sweden, and Russia. Cesare Beccaria, *Dei delitti e delle pene* (1764), ed. Franco Venturi (Turin, 1965; 3rd ed., 1973); for a summary, see Venturi, *Utopia and Reform in the Enlightenment,* chap. 4. J. G. A. Pocock, *The Machiavellian Moment: Florentine Political Thought and the Atlantic Republican Tradition* (Princeton, N.J., 1975), and "*The Machiavellian Moment* Revisited: A Study in History and Ideology," *Journal of Modern History,* 53 (1981), 71.

10. Robert Darnton, *The Business of Enlightenment: A Publishing History of the* Encyclopédie, *1775–1800* (Cambridge, Mass., 1979), 530, chaps. 6, 10, apps. B, C, and "The *Encyclopédie* Wars

of Prerevolutionary France," *American Historical Review,* 78 (1973), 1346–52. Cf. François Furet et al., *Livre et société dans la France du XVIIe siècle,* 2 vols. (Paris, 1965–70).

11. Robert R. Palmer, *The Age of the Democratic Revolution,* 2 vols. (Princeton, N.J., 1959–64), and Jacques Godechot, *La grande nation: L'expansion révolutionnaire de la France dans le monde, de 1789 à 1799,* 2 vols. (Paris, 1956). On Populism as a movement "on the fringe of the metropolitan culture," see James Turner, "Understanding the Populists," *Journal of American History,* 67 (1980–81), esp. 370–71. For twelve wide-ranging essays applying this concept, see Jean Gottmann, ed., *Centre and Periphery: Spatial Variations in Politics* (Beverly Hills, Calif., 1980). On value systems and social organization, see Edward Shils, "Centre and Periphery," in *The Logic of Personal Knowledge* . . . (London [1961]), 117–30. For an attempt to use this concept to explain "capitalist agriculture and the origins of the European world-economy in the sixteenth century," see Immanuel Wallerstein, *The Modern World-System,* I (New York, 1974); in the second volume (New York, 1980), the same scheme is used in an effort to explain "mercantilism and the consolidation of the European world-economy, 1600–1750." For orbits of cultural dissemination, see, for example, Robert D. Mitchell, "The Formation of Early American Culture Regions: An Interpretation," in *European Settlement and Development in North America* . . . , ed. James R. Gibson (Toronto, 1978), 66–90; C. Lee Hopple, "Spatial Development of the Southeastern Pennsylvania Plain Dutch Community to 1970," *Pennsylvania Folklife,* 21 (1971–72), no. 2, 14–40, and no. 3, 36–45.

[Since 1981 the spatial expansion of the subjects of inquiry has developed to an extraordinary degree. It has been enriched and elaborated not because of the rising interest in global phenomena but because of the growing awareness of the importance of large-scale, subglobal regional units connected to the wider world but discrete in themselves. The history of one such regional area has been at the center of my own work for many years in the form of a long-term project on Atlantic history—the study of the transnational, comparative, and interactive history of the people of the four Atlantic continents. The project—the Atlantic History Seminar at Harvard University—has involved research of my own, summarized in *Atlantic History: Concepts and Contours* (2005) and a program for young historians from the four continents that involved annual seminars, workshops, conferences, and publications. The details of the work of the program are available in the Atlantic History's website, http://www.fas.harvard .edu/~atlantic/. Similar projects on Atlantic history have developed elsewhere in the United States, and in Canada, Britain, France, and Germany.

Other transnational oceanic regions have also been the subjects of historical inquiries, especially the Mediterranean world and more recently the Indian Ocean area and the Pacific region. The broader, more general study of regionalism in the contemporary world—geopolitical and economic—has also flourished since the 1990s: Louise Fawcett and Andrew Hurrell, *Regionalism in World Politics* (1995); "AHR Forum: Bringing Regionalism Back to History," *American Historical Review*, 104, no. 4 (1999); Louise Fawcett, "Exploring Regional Domains: A Comparative History of Regionalism," *International Affairs*, 80, no. 2 (2004).]

12. William L. Langer, "The Next Assignment," *American Historical Review*, 63 (1957–58), 283–304.

13. Gordon J. Schochet, *Patriarchalism in Political Thought* (New York, 1975), esp. chaps. 3, 4; W. H. Greenleaf, *Order, Empiricism, and Politics: Two Traditions of English Political Thought, 1500–1700* (London, 1964). For a review of such writings

on American themes, see Robert E. Shalhope, "Toward a Republican Synthesis: The Emergence of an Understanding of Republicanism in American Historiography," *William and Mary Quarterly,* 3rd ser., 29 (1972), 49–80.

14. Carl E. Schorske, *Fin-de-Siècle Vienna: Politics and Culture* (New York, 1980); William J. McGrath, *Dionysian Art and Populist Politics in Austria* (New Haven, Conn., 1974).

15. Natalie Zemon Davis, *Society and Culture in Early Modern France* (Stanford, Calif., 1975), chap. 4; Rhys Isaac, "Dramatizing the Ideology of Revolution: Popular Mobilization in Virginia, 1774–1776," *William and Mary Quarterly,* 3d ser., 33 (1976), 357–85; John Brewer, "Theatre and Counter-Theatre in Georgian Politics: The Mock Election at Garrat," *Radical History Review,* 22 (1979–80), 7–40.

16. Theodore Zeldin, *France, 1848–1945,* 2 vols. (Oxford, 1973–77), I, 2, 8; Guy Thuillier, *Pour une histoire du quotidien au XIXe siècle en Nivernais* (Paris, 1977); Norman Cohn, *The Pursuit of the Millennium* (New York, 1957); Perry Miller, *The New England Mind: The Seventeenth Century* (Cambridge, Mass., 1939), and *The New England Mind: From Colony to Province* (Cambridge, Mass., 1953); Keith Thomas, *Religion and the Decline of Magic* (London, 1971); Alan Macfarlane, *Witchcraft in Tudor and Stuart England* (London, 1970). See also Emmanuel Le Roy Ladurie, *Montaillou* (Paris, 1976), trans. Barbara Bray (London, 1978).

17. On Lamprecht, see Karl J. Weintraub, *Visions of Culture* (Chicago, 1966), 167, chap. 4; and Annie M. Popper, "Karl Lamprecht," in *Some Historians of Modern Europe,* ed. Bernadotte Schmitt (Chicago, 1942), 217–39. Lamprecht's ideas, which created a storm in Germany, were rejected there and his prodigious efforts (including his twenty-one-volume *Deutsche Geschichte*) written off as a tissue of errors, hopelessly schematic and methodologically unsound. But he was honored by historians in the United States, who found (in the broadly based psychogenetic *Kulturgeschichte* he advocated and wrote) elements of the reform program that would become known

as the New History. (The name itself seems to have originated in a favorable review essay: E. W. Dow, "Features of the New History: Apropos of Lamprecht's 'Deutsche Geschichte,'" *American Historical Review*, 3 [1897–98], 431–48.) Carl Becker was particularly intrigued and puzzled by Lamprecht's ideas. They seemed to support his interest in climates of opinion but yet to verge on sheer fancy. Lamprecht's concentration on the "one common underlying psychic mechanism" in the histories of nations and cultures, Becker wrote, threatened to transform the real substance of history into "social experience deposited in nerve centers." Becker, "Some Aspects of the Influence of Social Problems and Ideas upon the Study and Writing of History," *American Journal of Sociology*, 18 (1913), 673–74. [Cf. Roger Chickering, *Karl Lamprecht: A German Academic Life (1856–1915)* (Atlantic Highlands, N.J., 1993).]

18. Robert W. Fogel, " 'Scientific' History and Traditional History," in *Logic, Methodology, and the Philosophy of Science*, ed. L. J. Cohen et al., VI (Amsterdam, 1980). Cf. Robert William Fogel and G. A. Elton, *Which Road to the Past?: Two Views of History* (New Haven, Conn., 1983).

[Since Fogel's time the most original and elaborate approach to the relation of history and the sciences is the "Initiative for the Science of the Human Past," a large-scale project initiated and directed by Professor Michael McCormick at Harvard. Bringing the knowledge and skills of senior specialists in all areas of the sciences—molecular geneticists, biologists, anthropologists, chemists, climatologists, linguists, astronomers, and atmospheric scientists—to focus on deep-lying historical problems, McCormick hopes "to remake our understanding of the human past." The project's first experiments and products have been impressive: DNA studies of the Black Death and the Justinian pandemic; isotopes to trace a significant shift in the diet of working-class people in

Italy, 600–1500; chemical analysis of Carolingian coins; volcanoes and economic changes in Europe; and a multiscientific study of the remains of a royal estate near Bruges and a late Roman settlement in eastern France, involving radiocarbon dating, ground-penetrating radar, chemical trace element analysis, soil nanostructures, and micromorphology. But the basic purpose of McCormick's extraordinary scientific-humanist venture is not to transform history into a science but to mobilize science to help explain, at a profoundly latent level, what human life has been and to contribute new clarity, depth, and detail to the essential story of how we became the people we are and what the circumstances have been that have shaped our lives.]

4.

HISTORY AND THE CREATIVE IMAGINATION

Perry Miller

WORKS CITED

ed. (with Thomas H. Johnson), *The Puritans* (New York, 1938)

The New England Mind: The Seventeenth Century (Cambridge, Mass., 1939)

Jonathan Edwards (New York, 1949)

The New England Mind: From Colony to Province (Cambridge, Mass., 1953)

Errand into the Wilderness (Cambridge, Mass., 1956)

Nature's Nation (Cambridge, Mass., 1967)

CURRENT BIOGRAPHY

Edmund S. Morgan, "Perry Miller and the Historians," *Proceedings of the American Antiquarian Society,* 74 (1965), 11–18.

David Hollinger, "Perry Miller and Philosophical History," *History and Theory,* 7 (1968), 189–202.

David D. Hall, Introduction, in Perry Miller, *Orthodoxy in Massachusetts, 1630–1650* (New York, Torchbook ed., 1970), vii–xxiv.

James Hoopes, "Art as History: Perry Miller's *New England Mind,*" *American Quarterly,* 34 (1982), 3–25.

Francis T. Butts, "The Myth of Perry Miller," *American Historical Review,* 87 (1982), 665–94.

Randall Fuller, "Errand into the Wilderness: Perry Miller as American Scholar," *American Literary History,* 18 (2006), 102–28.

Charles McLean Andrews

WORKS CITED

The Colonial Period of American History, 4 vols. (New Haven, Conn., 1934–38)

"On the Writing of Colonial History," *William and Mary Quarterly,* 3rd ser., 1 (1944), 27–48.

CURRENT BIOGRAPHY

A. S. Eisenstadt, *Charles McLean Andrews* (New York, 1956)

Bernard Bailyn, "Becker, Andrews, and the Image of Colonial Origins," *New England Quarterly,* 29, no. 4 (1956), 522–34.

Lewis Namier

WORKS CITED

The Structure of Politics at the Accession of George III, 2 vols. (London, 1929)

England in the Age of the American Revolution (London, 1930)

CURRENT BIOGRAPHY

Julia Namier, *Lewis Namier: A Biography* (London, 1971)

J. H. Plumb, "Sir Lewis Namier," in *The Making of an Historian* (Athens, 1988), 10–19.

Linda Colley, *Lewis Namier* (London, 1989)

Ronald Syme

WORKS CITED

The Roman Revolution (Oxford, 1939)

Tacitus, 2 vols. (Oxford, 1958)

Colonial Élites: Rome, Spain, and the Americas (London, 1958)

G. W. Bowersock, "The Emperor of Roman History," *New York Review of Books,* March 6, 1980.

———, "Ronald Syme, 1903–1989," *Proceedings of the British Academy,* 84 (1994), 539–63.

5.

THE LOSERS

1. Mercy Otis Warren, *History of the Rise, Progress and Termination of the American Revolution . . . ,* 3 vols. (Boston, 1805); David Ramsay, *History of the American Revolution,* 2 vols. (Philadelphia, 1789); William Gordon, *The History of the Rise, Progress, and Establishment of the Independence of the United States of America . . . ,* 4 vols. (London, 1788). (A three-volume American edition was printed in New York, 1789 and following.) Gordon's *History* was published in London, where friends and booksellers warned him that his wild praise of the Americans and his fierce condemnation of Britain had to be moderated if the book were to sell. Though he did accordingly tone down the book's "spirit," it still retains its original polemical style. George W. Pilcher, "William Gordon and the History of the American Revolution," *The Historian* (1972), 453.

2. Douglass Adair and John A. Schutz, eds., *Peter Oliver's Origin & Progress of the American Rebellion: A Tory View* (San Marino, Calif., 1961), xii.

3. Peter Oliver's New York equivalent, the colony's supreme court justice Thomas Jones, wrote in his Hertfordshire exile a history that parallels Oliver's for events in New York, but it emerged into print only in 1879 and then in a somewhat watered-down version prepared by a judicious descendant (Thomas Jones, *History of New York during the Revolutionary War . . . ,* ed. Edward F. de Lancey, 2 vols., New York, 1879). The hundred-page introduction the exiled Maryland preacher Jonathan Boucher composed in 1797 for an edition of his

collected sermons does constitute a contemporary counter-interpretation of sorts, but it was written to capitalize on the public interest in the French not the American Revolution, and its point is therefore diffused; it did not sketch out a useful counter-interpretation (Jonathan Boucher, *A View of the Causes and Consequences of the American Revolution . . . ,* London, 1797). And Joseph Galloway's *Historical and Political Reflections on the Rise and Progress of the American Rebellion . . .* (London, 1780), though it is in part an historical interpretation of the origins of the Revolution, is mainly a polemical pamphlet "written in great haste, amidst a multiplicity of other engagements." It is one of four pamphlets Galloway published in 1779 and 1780 in which he continued to promote the plan of union he had first proposed in 1774 and carried forward his condemnation of General William Howe and Admiral Lord Richard Howe for having blundered inexcusably in the military campaigns of 1775 and 1776. The pamphlet was lost among the polemical writings of the time and had no impact on the development of historical ideas. Julian P. Boyd, *Anglo-American Union: Joseph Galloway's Plans to Preserve the British Empire, 1774–1788* (Philadelphia, 1941), 102.

4. Thomas Hutchinson, *The History of the Colony and Province of Massachusetts-Bay,* 3 vols., ed. Lawrence S. Mayo (Cambridge, Mass., 1936).

An unreliable epitome of the exiled Judge Samuel Curwen's *Journal and Letters* was published by his great-grandnephew George A. Ward in London in 1842 (the later editions of this book—1844, 1845, 1864—did not improve the text). The whole of Curwen's voluminous and revealing journal reached print only in 1972 in a meticulous edition prepared by Andrew Oliver (2 vols., Cambridge, Mass.). William Smith's important journals and papers are still not fully published. One segment of the manuscripts in the New York Public Library has appeared as a two-volume mimeographed typescript, edited by William H. W. Sabine, privately distributed, the first volume (1956) covering the period March 16, 1763, to July 9, 1776, the second (1958) covering July 12, 1776, to July 25, 1778; a later segment has been better served: L. F. S. Upton, ed., *The Diary and Selected Papers of Chief Justice William Smith, 1784–1793,* 2 vols. (Toronto, 1963–65). Jonathan Boucher's *Reminiscences of an American Loyalist, 1738–1789* appeared only in 1925 in an edition prepared by his grandson, Jonathan Bouchier, and his letters were printed only in 1912 and 1913 in various issues of the *Maryland Historical Magazine.*

5. George Otto Trevelyan, *The American Revolution, Part II* (London, 1903), II, 241, 239, 240 (pronouns in the Selwyn quotation made consistently plural); Curwen, *Journal,* I, 284.

6. John Adolphus, *History of England from the Accession of King George the Third to the Conclusion of the Peace . . .* (London, 1802), II, 66, 172, 176, 406, 408.

7. Cf. Herbert Butterfield, *George III and the Historians* (London, 1957), 62–63.

8. Lord Mahon (later, Fifth Earl Stanhope), *History of England from the Peace of Utrecht to the Peace of Versailles, 1713–1783* [1836–54] (3rd ed., Boston, 1854), VI, 99–106, 7.

9. It was not until 1911 that an English historian, Henry Belcher (fellow of King's College, London, and rector at Lewes, Sussex, with access to the Gage Papers there), set out to defend the crown from the "high lights and dark shadows invented by Whig disciples of Clio on either shore of the Atlantic," and in doing so wrote an account almost entirely from the loyalists' point of view. But his two-volume work, significantly entitled *The First American Civil War,* is poorly composed, covers only the years 1775–78, and is tangled in an overambitious effort to combine social, political, and military history; it was nothing to put against the lucidity of the works of G. O. Trevelyan and W. E. H. Lecky, which by then had set the major lines of interpretation for this whole era of British history in terms that would survive in England without effective challenge until Lewis B. Namier published his epochal

volumes of 1929 and 1930: *The Structure of Politics at the Accession of George III* and *England in the Age of the American Revolution.* (See Essay 4, above.)

10. Trevelyan published seven volumes on the Revolutionary period: *The Early History of Charles James Fox* (London, 1880); *The American Revolution* (3 parts in 4 vols., London and New York, 1899–1907); and *George III and Charles James Fox* (2 vols., London and New York, 1912–14). For his treatment of the loyalists, see *American Revolution, Part II,* II, 231ff.; *Part III,* 347ff.

11. Lecky's *History* was published in eight volumes, London, 1878–90. The sections on the American Revolution, in the third and fourth volumes, were extended, edited, and published as a separate book by James A. Woodburn: *The American Revolution, 1763–1783, Being the Chapters and Passages Relating to America from [Lecky's] History of England in the Eighteenth Century* (New York and London, 1898).

12. Lecky, *History,* III, 443, 414, 418, 354, 361.

13. Lecky himself in his later years became increasingly alienated from contemporary society, more conservative and antidemocratic. For Fisher's articles cited, see *Forum,* 14 (January 1893), 608–15; *Appleton's Popular Science Monthly,* 49 (September 1896), 625–30; *Forum,* 16 (January 1894), 560–67; *Appleton's Popular Science Monthly,* 48 (December 1895–January 1896), 244–55; [Lawrence H. Gipson], "Sydney George Fisher," *Dictionary of American Biography,* VI, 411–12.

14. Henry W. Haynes, "Memoir of Mellen Chamberlain," *Proceedings of the Massachusetts Historical Society,* 2nd ser., 20 (1906–7), 119–46.

15. O. B. Frothingham, "Memoir of George Edward Ellis, D.D., LL.D.," *Proceedings of the Massachusetts Historical Society,* 2nd ser., 10 (1895–96), 207–55; and remarks of C. F. Adams et al., ibid., 9 (1894–95), 244ff. (esp. 253).

16. Sydney George Fisher, *Men, Women and Manners in Colonial Times,* 2nd ed. (Philadelphia and London, 1898), I, 72, 75–77, 97; *True History of the American Revolution* (Philadelphia, 1902),

chap. viii, 165; *Struggle for American Independence* (Philadelphia and London, 1908), I, chaps. xxi, xxii.

17. Sydney George Fisher, "The Legendary and Myth-Making Process in Histories of the American Revolution," *Proceedings of the American Philosophical Society,* 51 (April–June 1912), 53–75.

18. George E. Ellis, "Governor Thomas Hutchinson," *Atlantic Monthly,* 53 (1884), 665, 675, 676, 667, 669.

19. George E. Ellis, "The Loyalists and Their Fortunes," in *Narrative and Critical History of America,* ed. Justin Winsor (Boston and New York, 1884–89), VII, 192–93.

20. For Chamberlain's views of the loyalists and for his understanding of the role of the Revolution in American history, see his "The Revolution Impending," in Winsor, *Narrative and Critical History,* VI, chap. i, and his "Address," in *John Adams . . . with Other Essays . . .* (Boston and New York, 1898), 429ff.

21. [Solon J. Buck], "James Kendall Hosmer," *Dictionary of American Biography,* IX, 244–45; James K. Hosmer, *A Short History of Anglo-Saxon Freedom* (New York, 1890), ix–x, 219–21, 225–30, 222. Apparently Hosmer drew the attractive idea that the Revolution had really been a war between Englishmen and Germans, rather than between Englishmen and Americans, from an article by O. J. Casey, "Anglophobia in the United States," *Westminster Review,* 131 (1889), 328, itself a reply to a belligerently anti-American article of the same title that had appeared in the *Review* the year before (vol. 130, 736–56).

22. Hosmer, *Anglo-Saxon Freedom,* 225, 228, 229, 230–31.

23. Hosmer, *The Life of Young Sir Henry Vane . . .* (Boston and New York, 1888); *The Life of Thomas Hutchinson . . .* (Boston and New York, 1896), [xiii], 349; *Samuel Adams* (Boston and New York, 1885), 281.

24. Abner C. Goodell Jr., in *American Historical Review,* 2 (1896–97), 163–70 (on Goodell—"in matters historical, he lacked all sense of proportion . . . his [death] now causes in us no sense of immediate loss"—see *Proceedings of the Massachusetts Histori-*

cal Society, 48 [1914–15], 5, 6); [Moses Coit Tyler], *Nation,* 62 (March 26, 1896), 258–59; Howard Mumford Jones, *Life of Moses Coit Tyler* (Ann Arbor, Mich., 1933), 266. Hosmer sent a copy of the book to Peter Orlando Hutchinson, Hutchinson's great-grandson, the editor of his *Diary and Letters,* who was then in his eighty-sixth year. Hutchinson responded, March 18, 1896 (Misc. Bound MSS, Massachusetts Historical Society), in a warm letter of thanks, describing his long years of work preserving and editing the papers that were in the governor's possession when he died and his final sale of the fourteen volumes to the British Museum for £100.

25. Moses Coit Tyler, "On Certain English Hallucinations Touching America," in *Glimpses of England* (New York and London, 1898), 279, 283–85; Andrew D. White to W. E. H. Lecky, July 30, 1890, in [Elisabeth Lecky], *A Memoir of . . . Lecky . . .* (New York and London, 1909), 186; Jones, *Tyler,* 258; Tyler, *Literary History of the American Revolution, 1763–1783* (New York and London, 1897), I, chaps. xiii–xvii; II, chaps. xxvii–xxix; Charles Kendall Adams to Tyler, July 30, 1897, in Jessica T. Austen, ed., *Moses Coit Tyler, 1833–1900: Selections from His Letters and Diaries* (Garden City, N.Y., 1911), 295–96. For Lecky's appreciation of Tyler's book, see ibid., 300–301.

26. W. E. H. Lecky, *Historical and Political Essays* (London, 1908; reprinted Freeport, N.Y., 1970), 64.

27. Herbert L. Osgood, "The Study of American Colonial History," *Annual Report of the American Historical Association for the Year 1898* (Washington, D.C., 1899), 72; A. S. Eisenstadt, *Charles McLean Andrews* (New York, 1956), chap. v; George Louis Beer, *British Colonial Policy, 1754–1765* (New York, 1907), 315–16; Beer, *The English-Speaking Peoples* (New York, 1917), x, ix.

28. Lawrence Henry Gipson, *The British Empire Before the American Revolution* (Caldwell, Idaho, and New York, 1936–70) I, vii; Gipson, *Jared Ingersoll: A Study of American Loyalism in Relation to British Colonial Government* (New Haven, Conn., 1920).

29. Wallace Brown, *The King's Friends: The Composition and Motives of the American Loyalist Claimants* (Providence, R.I., 1965).

6.

THOMAS HUTCHINSON IN CONTEXT:
THE ORDEAL REVISITED

1. Peter O. Hutchinson, ed., *The Diary and Letters of His Excellency Thomas Hutchinson, Esq. . . . ,* 2 vols. (Boston and London, 1884–86), II, 194. For Hutchinson's interest in French and Japanese history, see *The Ordeal of Thomas Hutchinson* (Cambridge, Mass., 1974), 28, n. 46.

2. John Adams to Joseph Ward, October 24, 1809, in *Journal and Letters of the late Samuel Curwen . . . ,* ed. George Ward (3rd ed., New York, 1845), 456; *Ordeal of Thomas Hutchinson,* 27, nn. 44–45. For a more critical view of Hutchinson's judicial career, stressing the political slant of his Superior Court decisions, see John A. Denehy, "Thomas Hutchinson: Chief Justice of the Massachusetts Superior Court of Judicature," *Massachusetts Legal History,* 8 (2002), 1–34.

3. John Gardiner, quoted in Timothy A. Milford, "Advantage: The Gardiners and Anglo-America, 1750–1820" (Ph.D. diss., Harvard University, 1999), 35.

4. *The Spectator,* May 24, 1975; *Times Literary Supplement,* June 13, 1945. See also Franco Venturi, *The End of the Old Regime in Europe, 1768–1776: The First Crisis* [1979], trans. R. Burr Litchfield, (Princeton, N.J., 1989), 382.

5. John P. Reid, ed., *The Briefs of the American Revolution: Constitutional Arguments Between Thomas Hutchinson, Governor of Massachusetts Bay, and James Bowdoin for the Council and John Adams for the House of Representatives* (New York, 1981); cf. *Ordeal of Thomas Hutchinson,* chap. 6 ("The Failure of Reason"), esp. 207–11.

6. Paul Langford et al., eds., *The Writings and Speeches of Edmund Burke,* 9 vols. (Oxford, 1980–91), II, 458.

7. H. H. Gerth and C. Wright Mills, eds. and trans., *From Max*

Weber: Essays in Sociology (New York, 1958), 78; Catherine Barton Mayo, ed., "Additions to Thomas Hutchinson's 'History of Massachusetts Bay,'" *Proceedings of the American Antiquarian Society,* 59 (1949), 57.

8. *Ordeal of Thomas Hutchinson,* 236, 227.

9. Ibid., 242–43.

10. Ibid., 251.

11. Daniel J. Hulsebosch, "The Ancient Constitution and the Expanding Empire: Sir Edward Coke's British Jurisprudence," *Law and History Review,* 21 (2003), 446, 457, 458, 481.

12. Bernard Bailyn, ed., " 'A Dialogue between an American and a European Englishman' (1768), by Thomas Hutchinson," *Perspectives in American History,* 9 (1975), 365, 362.

13. *Ordeal of Thomas Hutchinson,* 380.

14. Ibid., 17.

15. John Adams to Abigail Adams, July 3, 1776, in *Adams Family Correspondence*, ed. L. H. Butterfield et al., 11 vols. (Cambridge, Mass., 1963–), II, 30.

7.
ENGLAND'S CULTURAL PROVINCES:
SCOTLAND AND AMERICA

1. P. Hume Brown, *Surveys of Scottish History* (Glasgow, 1919), 131.

2. Dugald Stewart, "Account of the Life and Writings of Adam Smith, LL.D.," in *The Collected Works of Dugald Stewart, Esq., F.R.S.E.,* ed. William Hamilton (Edinburgh, 1854–60), X, 82.

3. Robert Wodrow, *Analecta* (Edinburgh, 1842–43), IV, 185.

4. A reevaluation of Scottish cultural history in the two or three decades just before the Union of 1707 is especially desirable. Henry W. Meikle, *Some Aspects of Later Seventeenth Century Scotland* (Glasgow, 1947), was a step in the right direction. Detailed study of the church, the bar, and the University of Edinburgh around the turn of the century shows that a spirit of increasing tolerance and ever-broadening intellectual and

cultural interests had by then invaded all three of these institutions to a considerable degree.

5. George S. Gordon, *Anglo-American Literary Relations* (Oxford, 1942), 27.

6. Henry W. Foote, *John Smibert, Painter* (Cambridge, Mass., 1950), 60, 61.

7. Carl Bridenbaugh, ed., *Gentleman's Progress: The Itinerarium of Dr. Alexander Hamilton, 1744* (Chapel Hill, N.C., 1948), 186; Frederick A. Pottle, ed., *Boswell on the Grand Tour: Germany and Switzerland, 1764* (New York, 1953), 259.

8. Albert F. Gegenheimer, *William Smith* (Philadelphia, 1943), chaps. I–IV; Herbert and Carol Schneider, eds., *Samuel Johnson* (New York, 1929), I, 57; Arthur W. H. Eaton, *The Famous Mather Byles* (Boston, 1914), 101–3, 232–33.

9. Cadwallader Colden to the Earl of Halifax, February 22, 1765, quoted in Paul M. Hamlin, *Legal Education in Colonial New York* (New York, 1939), 37.

10. Carl Bridenbaugh, *Myths and Realities: Societies of the Colonial South* (Baton Rouge, La., 1952), 12, 17, 51, 52, 53.

11. Ibid., 65, 99, 117.

12. Henry Grey Graham, *The Social Life of Scotland in the Eighteenth Century*, 4th ed. (London, 1937), 33.

13. Harold W. Thompson, *A Scottish Man of Feeling* (New York, 1931), 34–35.

14. The list, dated October 17, 1759, is printed in Dugald Stewart, "Account of the Life and Writings of William Robertson, D.D.," *Works*, X, 205–7. The Reverend Alexander Carlyle, who supplied Stewart with it, notes in his *Autobiography* (Edinburgh, 1910), 311–12, that it is incomplete. But he lists only two additional members, one of them a lawyer.

15. S. G. Kermack, "Natural Jurisprudence and Philosophy of Law," in *An Introductory Survey of the Sources and Literature of Scots Law* (Edinburgh, 1936), 441.

16. William R. Scott, *Adam Smith as Student and Professor* (Glasgow, 1937), 55–61.

17. Thomas Newte, *Prospects and Observations on a Tour in England and Scotland* (London, 1791), 364.

18. John Chamberlayne, *Magnae Britanniae Notitia: Or, the Present State of Great Britain* (London, 1708), iii.

19. Perry Miller, *The New England Mind: From Colony to Province* (Cambridge, Mass., 1953), 6.

20. Wodrow, *Analecta*, III, 515.

21. William Eddis, *Letters from America . . . 1769 to 1777, inclusive* (London, 1792), quoted in Michael Kraus, *The Atlantic Civilization: Eighteenth-Century Origins* (Ithaca, N.Y., 1949), 37. Cf. Mr. Bramble's comment in *Humphry Clinker,* "A burgher of Edinburgh, not content to vie with a citizen of London, who has ten times his fortune, must excel him in the expence as well as elegance of his entertainments."

22. David Hume to John Clephane, April 20, 1756, in *The Letters of David Hume,* ed. J. Y. T. Greig (Oxford, 1932), I, 229; Adam Smith to Lord Fitzmaurice, February 21, 1759, quoted in Scott, *Adam Smith as Student and Professor,* 241.

23. John Winthrop Jr., to Henry Oldenburg, November 12, 1668, *Winthrop Papers,* Part IV, in Massachusetts Historical Society, *Collections,* 5th ser., VIII (1882), 131; J. S. Copley to Benjamin West, November 12, 1766, *Letters and Papers of John Singleton Copley and Henry Pelham, 1739–1776,* in Massachusetts Historical Society, *Collections,* LXXI (1914), 51.

24. George Dempster to Adam Fergusson, December 5, 1756, in *Letters of George Dempster to Sir Adam Fergusson, 1756–1813,* ed. James Fergusson (London, 1934), 15.

25. John Witherspoon, "The Druid, No. V [1781]," reprinted in *The Beginnings of American English,* ed. M. M. Mathews (Chicago, 1931), 17; G. Birkbeck Hill, ed., *Boswell's Life of Johnson* (New York, 1891), II, 184.

26. John Oxenbridge, *New-England Freemen Warned and Warmed . . .* ([Cambridge], 1673), 19.

27. John Ramsay, *Scotland and Scotsmen in the Eighteenth Century,* ed. Alexander Allardyce (Edinburgh, 1888), I, 5.

28. William Robertson to Baron Mure, November, 1761, Dugald Stewart, "Life of Robertson," 136; David Hume to Adam Fergusson, November 9, 1763, *Letters of David Hume,* I, 410–11.

29. William Tod to William Smellie, November 29, 1759, in *Memoirs of the Life, Writings, and Correspondence of William Smellie,* ed. Robert Kerr (Edinburgh, 1811), I, 46.

30. Frederick A. Pottle, ed., *Boswell's London Journal, 1762–1763* (New York, 1950), 71; Frederick A. Pottle, ed., *Boswell in Holland, 1763–1764* (New York, 1952), 137, 260.

[In recent years the relations of Scotland and America have been the subject of extensive study, which began with Andrew Hook's book *Scotland and America* (Glasgow, 1975). Among the notable studies that followed are: Alan Gailey, *Scotland, Ireland and America: Migrant Culture in the 17th and 18th Centuries* (Boston, 1984); Daniel Walker Howe, "Why the Scottish Enlightenment Was Useful to the Framers of the American Constitution," *Comparative Studies in Society and History,* 31, no. 3 (July 1989), 572–87; Richard B. Sher and Jeffrey R. Smitten, eds., *Scotland and America in the Age of the Enlightenment* (Edinburgh, 1990); Michael Fry et al., *Scotland and the Americas, 1600–1800* (Providence, R.I., 1995); Ned Landsman, ed., *Nation and Province in the First British Empire: Scotland and the Americas, 1600–1800* (Lewisburg, Pa., 2001); Richard B. Sher, *The Enlightenment and the Book: Scottish Authors and Their Publishers in Eighteenth-Century Britain, Ireland, and America* (Chicago, 2006); Elaine Breslaw, *Dr. Alexander Hamilton and Provincial America: Expanding the Orbit of Scottish Culture* (Baton Rouge, La., 2008); Alexander Murdoch, *Scotland and America, c.1600–c.1800* (New York, 2010). The most recent publications have gone further afield, into the relations between the two peoples as part of the transnational Atlantic complex. That broader subject has been surveyed and interpreted with great skill by Jose R. Torre, *William and Mary Quarterly*, 3rd ser., 65, no. 4 (October 2008), 801–13.]

8.

PEOPLING THE PERIPHERIES

[This essay, delivered at the Australian Academy of the Humanities, Canberra, was published as a pamphlet without annotation. I make no attempt now to annotate the text, which is the product of decades of research and reading in early North American history and the histories of Canada, Ireland, the British Caribbean islands, and Australia. But two of my books on which I particularly relied in writing the piece cover significant parts of the essay and contain full annotation of the sources: *The Peopling of British North America: An Introduction* (New York, 1986) and *Voyagers to the West: A Passage in the Peopling of America on the Eve of the Revolution* (New York, 1986). I cite here only direct quotations and a few less familiar works, important at distinctive points in the story.]

1. Joyce Chaplin, *Subject Matter: Technology, the Body, and Science on the Anglo-American Frontier, 1500–1675* (Cambridge, Mass., 2001), 115, 159–60, 186–91.

2. Sylvia Van Kirk, *Many Tender Ties: Women in Fur Trade Society, 1670–1870* (Norman, Okla., 1983).

3. Lord Adam Gordon, "Journal of an Officer . . . in 1764 and 1765," in *Travels in the American Colonies,* ed. Newton D. Mereness (New York, 1916), 417.

4. Quoted in Bernard Bailyn, *Voyagers to the West,* 449.

5. Alexander Grant to [Gov. James Grant], London, June 19, 1767, Macpherson-Grant Papers, bundle 402, Ballindalloch Castle, Scotland.

6. Stephen S. Webb, *The Governors General: The English Army and the Definition of the Empire, 1569–1681* (Chapel Hill, N.C., 1979), esp. chap. i.

7. William Stith, *The History of the First Discovery and Settlement of Virginia* . . . [1747], facsimile ed. (Spartanburg, S.C., 1965), 168; A. Roger Ekirch, *Bound for America: The Transportation of British Convicts to the Colonies, 1718–1775* (Oxford, 1987), 116, 142; Charles Bateson, *The Convict Ships, 1787–1868* (2nd ed., Glasgow, 1969), app. VII; A. G. L. Shaw, *Convicts and the Colonies* (Melbourne, 1966), 149. I am greatly indebted to Professor Alan Frost, La Trobe University, for his expert help in establishing the numbers of convicts sent to Australia. He is not responsible for what I have written here.

8. Alan Frost, *Arthur Phillip, 1738–1814: His Voyaging* (Melbourne, 1987), 202.

9. Portia Robinson, *The Hatch and Brood of Time: A Study of the First Generation of Native-Born White Australians, 1788–1828* (Melbourne, 1985), 6.

9.

THE SEARCH FOR PERFECTION:
ATLANTIC DIMENSIONS

1. Michael A. Ignatieff, *Isaiah Berlin: A Life* (London, 1998), 205.

2. Isaiah Berlin, "Notes on the Way," *Time and Tide* (November 12, 19, 26, 1949), quotations at 1133, 1157, 1158, 1188. Berlin's Harvard experience remained vivid in his memory. Thirty-five years later he recalled that "when I was at Harvard—it was exhausting, but it obliged one to think more than anything at Oxford or Cambridge has in my day." American students at Harvard and elsewhere, he wrote in 1987,

> believed that objective truth was discoverable; that the professor may well have possessed it; that with enough pressure he might reveal it; not much was understood of

selective and critical reading. But I used to recommend bibliographies—and students used to ask which chapters, or even sections, of these books they were to read, as they read every word, without skipping, without the slightest sense of what was important and what was not. Their search for the truth, their belief that anything new, or even true, was worth earnest endeavours to extract from the professor, was touching—and for the professor often rather moving and flattering, after the biases of English students. But in the end it turned out to be a little too naive—the graduates were sometimes very good at Harvard, the undergraduates seldom.

Berlin to Andrzej Walicki, April 22, 1985; April 21, 1987, *Dialogue and Universalism,* I–X (2005), 151, 155.

3. Bernard Bailyn et al., *Glimpses of the Harvard Past* (Cambridge, Mass., 1986), 13–18.
4. Leo Strauss, *The Rebirth of Classical Political Rationalism,* ed. Thomas L. Pangle (Chicago, 1989), xxviii, 16.
5. Isaiah Berlin, "Two Concepts of Liberty" [1958], in *Four Essays on Liberty* (London, 1969), 132–33, xliv, xlvii; "The Decline of Utopian Ideas in the West" [1978], in *The Crooked Timber of Humanity* (New York, 1991), 20–48, esp. 45–47; "The Pursuit of the Ideal," ibid., 18–19.
6. Ignatieff, *Berlin,* 234–36, 246–47, 253; Aurel Kolnai, *The Utopian Mind and Other Papers,* ed. Francis Dunlop (Atlantic Highlands, N.J., 1995), esp. 39–46, 69–86; Judith N. Shklar, "The Political Theory of Utopia: From Melancholy to Nostalgia" and "What Is the Use of Utopia?" in *Political Thought and Political Thinkers,* ed. Stanley Hoffmann (Chicago, 1998); George Kateb, comp., *Utopia* (New York, 1971); Melissa Lane, "Plato, Popper, Strauss, and Utopianism," *History of Philosophy Quarterly,* 16 (1999), 119–42; essays in *Daedalus,* 94 (1965), no. 2 ("Utopia"). Ian Harris lists the voluminous criticisms of and commentaries on the full range of Berlin's ideas in "Berlin and

His Critics," Isaiah Berlin, *Liberty,* ed. Henry Hardy (Oxford, 2002), [349]–66.

7. Quentin Skinner, "A Third Concept of Liberty," *Proceedings of the British Academy,* 117 (2002), 264.

8. Keith Thomas, "The Utopian Impulse in Seventeenth-Century England," in *Between Dream and Nature: Essays on Utopia and Dystopia,* ed. Dominic Baker-Smith and C. C. Barfoot (Amsterdam, 1987), 43, 24.

  Frank E. Manuel and Fritzie P. Manuel in their massive *Utopian Thought in the Western World* (Cambridge, Mass., 1979), 14–15, rule out any consideration of utopian ideas in the Americas because they were "derivative," mere "extensions of European idea systems," "the pabulum of an age, the chewed cud of previous epochs." Only in Europe, they write, were there "significant innovations," "new departures," "the major constellations of Utopian thought." In what follows I concentrate on precisely the two aspects of utopianism they dismiss: perfectionism in the Americas and the "chewed cud" of derivative ideas. My purpose is to trace the implementation of some of these ideas in the real and uniquely favorable conditions of colonial America and to consider some of the consequences. On the feverish utopianism of England, 1640–60, ibid., chap. xiii, esp. 334.

9. Ibid., "Introduction: The Utopian Propensity"; Thomas, "Utopian Impulse," 24, 31, 32. J. C. Davis, in *Utopia and the Ideal Society . . . 1516–1700* (Cambridge, England, 1981), chap. i, distinguishes utopian societies from four other types of ideal communities.

10. Manuel and Manuel, *Utopian Thought,* 334, 21–23.

11. John L. Phelan, *The Millennial Kingdom of the Franciscans in the New World . . .* (Berkeley, Calif., 1956), 73; Richard H. Popkin, "Hartlib, Dury, and the Jews," in *Samuel Hartlib and Universal Reformation,* ed. M. Greengrass et al. (Cambridge, England, 1994), 124–30; Champlin Burrage, "The Fifth Monarchy Insurrections," *English Historical Review,* 25 (1910), 739–47

("Fanatique" was Pepys's term); Philip F. Gura, *A Glimpse of Sion's Glory: Puritan Radicalism in New England, 1620–1660* (Middletown, Conn., 1984), 136–44.

12. Georges Baudot, *Utopia and History in Mexico . . . (1520–1569)*, trans. Bernard R. Ortiz de Montellano and Thelma Ortiz de Montellano (Niwot, Colo., 1995), chaps. v, vi.

13. Silvio Zavala, *Sir Thomas More in New Spain: A Utopian Adventure of the Renaissance (Diamante* no. 3) (London, 1955), 12; Zavala, "The American Utopia of the Sixteenth Century," *Huntington Library Quarterly,* 4 (1947), 341, 344–47; Fintan B. Warren, *Vasco de Quiroga and his Pueblo-Hospitals of Santa Fe* (Washington, D.C., 1963), 4–5, 29, 32–35, 116–17. On Quiroga's larger scheme for congregating all Amerindians into *repúblicas de indios,* and the details of the regulations in his hospital-*pueblos*: Bernardino Verástique, *Muchoacán and Eden: Vasco de Quiroga and the Evangelization of Western Mexico* (Austin, Tex., 2000), 120–40; James Holstun, *A Rational Millennium: Puritan Utopias of Seventeenth-Century England and America* (New York, 1987), 14.

14. Allan Greer and Kenneth Mills, "A Catholic Atlantic," in Jorge Cañizares-Esguerra and Erik R. Seeman, eds., *The Atlantic in Global History* (Upper Saddle River, N.J., 2006), 10. Barbara Ganson, *The Guarani Under Spanish Rule in the Rio de la Plata* (Stanford, Calif., 2003), chaps. ii, iii; José Gabriel Martinez-Serna, "Instruments of Empire: Jesuit-Indian Encounters in the New World Borderlands" (Working Paper, Atlantic History Seminar, Harvard University, 2004), 8–29; Philip Caraman, *The Lost Paradise: An Account of the Jesuits in Paraguay, 1607–1768* (London, 1975).

15. Theodore D. Bozeman, *To Live Ancient Lives . . .* (Chapel Hill, N.C., 1988), chap. iii; W. Clark Gilpin, *The Millenarian Piety of Roger Williams* (Chicago, 1979), 14; Cotton Mather, *The Wonders of the Invisible World . . .* (Boston, 1692), 6. Mather was referring to, and misreading, Budé's letter to Thomas Lupset, which first appeared as a preface to More's *Utopia* in 1517.

16. Edmund S. Morgan, *Roger Williams: The Church and the State* (New York, 1967), 4; Theodore D. Bozeman, *The Precisionist Strain* . . . (Chapel Hill, N.C., 2004), chap. ix, Part III. The most complete account of the great explosion of radical groups in early New England is Gura, *Sion's Glory:* on Münster and the Anabaptists as "incendiaries of commonwealths," 93, 115, 128, 256. On the Antinomian turmoil: Michael P. Winship, *Making Heretics: Militant Protestantism and Free Grace in Massachusetts, 1636–1641* (Princeton, N.J., 2002).

17. Sydney V. James, *Colonial Rhode Island: A History* (New York, 1975), 37.

18. William Hunt, *The Puritan Moment: The Coming of the Revolution in an English County* (Cambridge, Mass., 1983), 222–23; John Cotton, *A Reply to Mr. Williams . . . in The Bloudy Tenent, Washed and Made White . . .* (London, 1647), 5; Arthur Searle, " 'Overmuch Liberty': Roger Williams in Essex," *The Essex Journal,* 3 (1968), 85–92; Gura, *Sion's Glory,* 190.

19. Ibid., 217; Richard S. Dunn et al., eds., *The Journal of John Winthrop, 1630–1649* (Cambridge, Mass., 1996), 300; on the maturing of Williams's beliefs and his "obsession with personal and ecclesiastical purity," see Gilpin, *Millenarian Piety,* 50ff., and Morgan, *Williams.*

20. Richard W. Cogley, *John Eliot's Mission to the Indians Before King Philip's War* (Cambridge, Mass., 1999), 46, 251–52 (Cotton's lectures on Revelation); J. F. Maclear, "New England and the Fifth Monarchy: The Quest for the Millennium in Early American Puritanism," *William and Mary Quarterly,* 3rd ser., 32 (1975), 225, 231–34, 255; James Holstun, "John Eliot's Empirical Millenarianism," *Representations,* 4 (1983), 143, 145–46; Holstun, *Rational Millennium,* 104–9, 113–14.

21. Cogley, *Eliot's Mission,* 92–93, 79–81, 88, 90; Maclear, "New England and the Fifth Monarchy," 254–55, 229, 244–47; Holstun, *Rational Millennium,* 132, 115, 111–13 (on the relations of Eliot's utopianism to the classic utopias from Plato to Bacon and Comenius, 132–33, 157–58). On the belief that the Ameri-

can Indians were Jews from the lost tribes, and its significance to the millenarian thought of the Hartlib circle in England, see Richard Popkin's essay in Greengrass et al., eds., *Hartlib and Universal Reformation*, chap. v.

22. Holstun, *Rational Millennium*, 104, 131, 158; Holstun, "Eliot's Empirical Millenarianism," 131, 144, 147; Cogley, *Eliot's Mission*, 79.

23. Ibid., 165, 256–58, 114–16; Holstun, *Rational Millennium*, 159.

24. Leland Harder and Marvin Harder, *Plockhoy from Zurik-zee* (Newton, Kans., 1952), chap. ii; Davis, *Utopia*, 313–14, derived from Charles Webster's magisterial study of Hartlib and the world of utopian reform in all fields of learning, *The Great Instauration: Science, Medicine, and Reform, 1626–1660* (London, 1975).

25. Davis, *Utopia*, 313; Harder, *Plockhoy*, 28; Plockhoy to Cromwell [1659?], ibid., 120–30. Cf. Plockhoy to Cromwell, June 4, 1657, Hartlib Papers, Sheffield University Library, 54/23A–26B.

26. Plockhoy, *Way to Peace* and his *A Way Propounded to Make the Poor . . . Happy . . .* (London, 1659), in Harder and Harder, *Plockhoy*, 108 ff. and chap. vi.

27. Plockhoy to Cromwell [1659] in Harder and Harder, *Plockhoy*, 124; Hartlib to John Worthington, July 20, 1659, in *Diary and Correspondence of James Worthington*, ed. James Crossley et al. (Manchester, 1847–86), i, 156; Harder and Harder, *Plockhoy*, 37–41.

28. Ibid., 31–32; Davis, *Utopia*, 316, 338; Hartlib to Worthington, July 20, 1659, *Diary and Correspondence*, 156.

29. Hartlib to Worthington, October 15, 1660, ibid., 211; Harder and Harder, *Plockhoy*, 36, 48; Davis, *Utopia*, 313–14; Webster, *Instauration*, 98, 368. References to Virginia as a possible site for a utopian settlement abound in the Hartlib Papers; cf. Catherine Armstrong, "Antilia Revisited: Hartlib's Utopian Vision of America in Light of Recent Scholarship" (paper delivered at Birkbeck College conference, "New Worlds

Reflected: Representations of Utopia, the New World and Other Worlds (1500–1800)," December 2005). Cf. Donald R. Dickson, *The Tessera of Antilia* (Leiden, 1998), 118–25, 223–35, 251–56. The texts of Steendam's poems about New Netherland are in Henry C. Murphy, trans., *An Anthology of New Netherland . . .* (New York, 1865), [37]–75. On Plockhoy's brother Harmen: Peter S. Craig, "1671 Census of the Delaware," *Pennsylvania Genealogical Magazine*, 40 (1998), 358–59.

30. E. B. O'Callaghan et al., eds., *Documents Relative to the Colonial History of the State of New-York* (Albany, N.Y., 1856–87), II, 176; III, 346.

31. Elizabeth W. Fisher, " 'Prophecies and Revelations': German Cabbalists in Early Pennsylvania," *Pennsylvania Magazine of History and Biography*, 109 (1985), 299–333, and more generally Jon Butler, "Magic, Astrology, and the Early American Religious Heritage, 1600–1760," *American Historical Review*, 84 (1979), 317–46. Julius F. Sachse's antiquarian, anecdotal, rather chaotic *German Pietists of Provincial Pennsylvania* (Philadelphia, 1895), contains essential information.

32. Fisher, " 'Prophecies and Revelations,'" 319–24; Ernst L. Lashlee, "Johannes Kelpius and His Woman in the Wilderness," in *Glaube, Geist, Geschichte: Festschrift fur Ernst Benz,* ed. Gerhard Mueller and Winfried Zeller (Leiden, 1967), 327–31; Bernard Bailyn, *The Peopling of British North America: An Introduction* (New York, 1985), 123–27.

33. Julius F. Sachse, *The German Sectarians of Pennsylvania* (Philadelphia, 1899–1900) I, 73–77; Philip C. Croll, *Annals of the Oley Valley . . .* (Reading, Pa., 1926), chap. iii; Don Yoder, ed., *Rhineland Emigrants* (Baltimore, 1981), 99; Gillian L. Gollin, *Moravians in Two Worlds* (New York, 1967).

34. Samuel H. Brockunier, *The Irrepressible Democrat: Roger Williams* (New York, 1940), 283–89; Rivett, "Christian Transformations," 11; Edward G. Gray, *New World Babel: Languages and Nations in Early America* (Princeton, N.J., 1999), chap. iii; Kenneth L. Miner, "John Eliot of Massachusetts and the Begin-

nings of American Linguistics," *Historiographia Linguistica,* 1 (1974), 169–83; Stephen A. Guice, "The Linguistic Work of John Eliot" (Ph.D. diss., Michigan State University, 1990).

35. Davis, *Utopia,* 334–48; "P.B.," ed., *Industry Brings Plenty: John Bellers' Scheme for a Colledge of Industry* (London, 1916); Tim Hitchcock, "John Bellers," *Oxford Dictionary of National Biography* (Oxford, 2004); Robert Owen, *The Life of Robert Owen . . .* (London, 1857), 240; idem, *A Supplementary Appendix . . .* (London, 1858), reprints Bellers's *Colledge of Industry* and writes of Bellers, "Whatever merit can be due to an individual for the original discovery of a plan that, in its consequences, is calculated to effect more substantial and permanent benefit to mankind than any ever yet perhaps contemplated by the human mind, it all belongs exclusively to John Bellers"; Eduard Bernstein, *Cromwell and Communism: Socialism and Democracy in the Great English Revolution* [1895], trans. H. J. Stenning (London, 1930), chap. xv; Joshua Rowntree, *Social Service: Its Place in the Society of Friends* (London, 1913), 48–54; J. K. Fuz, *Welfare Economics in English Utopias . . .* (The Hague, 1952), 55–62; Jean Séguy, *Utopie coopérative et oecuménisme: Pieter Cornelisz Plockhoy van Zurick-Zee, 1620–1700* (Paris, 1968).

36. C. Lee Hopple, "Spatial Development of the Southeastern Pennsylvania Plain Dutch . . . ," *Pennsylvania Folklife,* 21 (1971–72), 18–20, 30–40; Yoder, *Rhineland Emigrants,* 99; Melvin E. Dieter, *The Holiness Revival of the Nineteenth Century* (Metuchen, N.J., 1980).

37. Berlin, "Two Concepts of Liberty," 119–21, 132.

Index

Index

Index

Bernard Bailyn did his undergraduate work at Williams College and his graduate work at Harvard University, where he is currently Adams University Professor and James Duncan Phillips Professor of Early American History, Emeritus. He founded, and for many years directed, the International Seminar on the History of the Atlantic World. Among his publications are *The Ideological Origins of the American Revolution*, which received the Pulitzer and Bancroft Prizes in 1968; *The Ordeal of Thomas Hutchinson*, which won the National Book Award for History in 1975; *Voyagers to the West*, which won the Pulitzer Prize in 1987; *To Begin the World Anew: The Genius and Ambiguities of the American Founders; Atlantic History: Concept and Contours;* and *The Barbarous Years: The Peopling of British North America: The Conflict of Civilizations, 1600–1675*. He served as the Jefferson Lecturer of the National Endowment for the Humanities and delivered the first Millennium Lecture at the White House. In 2010 he was awarded the National Humanities Medal.